UNCOMMON THREAD

All the Best!
Mary Ella
December 2013

UNCOMMON THREAD

A Woman, A Brand, A Legacy:
the Story of Peacock Alley Fine Linens

MARY ELLA GABLER

WITH DENISE GEE

FOREWORD BY ROGER HORCHOW

Text by Mary Ella Gabler with Denise Gee
Edited and Produced by Rebecca Sherman
Photography credits page 239
Book Design by Kristin Payne Atwell and Jon Binford
Copy Editing by Vince Scolaro
Cover Photograph Copyright © 2013 by Scogin Mayo

Some names and identifying details have been changed to protect the privacy of individuals.

Published by Peacock Alley
2050 Postal Way
Dallas, TX 75212
214.744.0399
www.peacockalley.com

Library of Congress Control Number: 2013912195
ISBN-13: 978-0-9896389-0-6

First Edition
Printed in Canada
10 9 8 7 6 5 4 3 2 1

FOR MY SONS
JASON AND JOSH

FOREWORD

In this day of multibillion-dollar conglomerates, merged department store names, disappearing familiar neighborhood shops and emerging retail merchandising stars, it is refreshing to have followed the career of Mary Ella Gabler from her early, happy days in Pennsylvania to her current happy days in Texas.

Now in the second decade of the 21st century, there are no longer retail icons like Stanley Marcus, Marshall Field, Fred Lazarus, Andrew Goodman, Marvin Traub. One would be hard pressed to name new "giants" of today's retail establishments.

However, in my opinion, the real standouts of our present retail environment are exemplified by Mary Ella and her Peacock Alley success. Her life history should be an inspiration to aspiring entrepreneurs because the frank and honest story of her struggles, successes and failures can't help but inspire others when they understand the full spectrum of this woman's career.

Ray Gabler and I worked together at Foley's in Houston in the 1950s. Ray became a supplier for my various retail departments, both at Neiman Marcus and at Horchow Collection, and later on Peacock Alley was an important supplier to the Horchow Collection.

So now we come full circle. And although my own career has changed, Mary Ella, with her fine family, has lived through feast and famine and emerged as one of the industry's most important interpreters of current trends in home furnishings. She understands her customers and elevates their tastes through her long experience in providing upscale, tasteful merchandise to a devoted following.

A great testament to Mary Ella is that she still supplies the vast majority of her original customers who were with her through good times and bad times. It will be a pleasure for you to be able to read and share this odyssey. I have enjoyed having a first-hand picture of this remarkable woman and her accomplishments.

—ROGER HORCHOW

1 COURAGE

Success is not final, failure is not fatal;
it is the courage to continue that counts.

—WINSTON CHURCHILL

I have a confession to make. Before I share it, though, you should know two things. I'm deeply, uncompromisingly passionate about luxury linens. Having adored beautifully made textiles from childhood, I've devoted 40 years to having Peacock Alley help others see just how soothing, elegant and complete our lives can be because of something so simple, yet so exquisite.

I've also accomplished a great deal in life—achieving the unthinkable, actually. I've plowed ahead in the face of adversity, adapted to ruthless competition, broken the proverbial glass ceiling in two different male-dominated industries, and done whatever necessary to keep moving forward—all thanks to a little boudoir pillow that led to a cottage industry that became a hugely successful business making bedding favored the world over, even for the Vatican. (How's that for a heavenly client?)

But here's what I really want you to know: I'd be lying to myself and you if this book painted a picture of my life as having been spent solely in the lap of luxury. That's not the case. I've been in the hot seat almost as many times as I've been in the catbird seat. All of this will be revealed in good time, but the important thing is that it will be revealed. Life is beautiful, yes, but life is also difficult.

The greatest conundrum is discussing anything negative while trying to be positive; it seems to go against my very nature. But negatives can be positives, at least when they strengthen you. Over the years I've decided it's best to be optimistic. So for the purpose of helping share the most important lessons I've learned in life, this book will revisit moments of grace, humor and loss so that we might all make our lives better.

Plenty of people believe I should have thrown in the towel (of the finest Egyptian cotton, no doubt) on several occasions. Ten years ago was one of them, an afternoon when, for the second time in my life, I found myself losing nearly everything I owned to pursue what I knew could succeed if given another chance: Peacock Alley.

This particular 2003 afternoon, I was in a bankruptcy attorney's office with our "work out" banker in charge of collecting on our business loan; two attorneys; my husband, Ray; my son Jason and a couple of financial advisers. All of us were gathered around a conference room table, and I was trying to think positively. Doing so had gotten me through the worst of times, which, from an accounting standpoint, had been experienced a decade earlier. Though the rebuilding process had been brutal, I had gotten through it. If anything, Peacock Alley and I rose from the ashes all the stronger. We had to be clever to survive. And we were.

But my present reality was this: A recession had led to a softening of our business, which might have been manageable had we put away enough savings. I had also just fired our CFO, and found myself caught in the midst of a creative retail gamble that we ultimately lost—to the tune of every liquid asset I owned. The fact I'm writing this book should be an indicator that I would fight like hell to rebuild, which I did. That story will unfold in the pages that follow. But at that moment, how we would rebuild wouldn't be clear. If anything it was a blur.

As the necessary paperwork for signing and initialing was collected and distributed, I gazed out at the city's sparkling skyscrapers, doing my best to stay calm and composed. As I often do when in deep thought, I found myself studying design—in this case, the uniqueness of the buildings' sharp points and soft curves, along with the coldness and tasteless interior of the room.

Ray, who knew me well enough to see what I was thinking (or trying not to think), reached for my hand and gave it a squeeze. I turned to respond with my eyes, which I did. But in the harsh light of the midday

PAGE 010) Peacock Alley's Vienna matelassé.
LEFT) Amish countryside in western Pennsylvania where my mother grew up.

sun streaming through the windows, I could also see how much Ray had aged during the past six months' struggle through what had not been Peacock Alley's finest hour. I wondered if that stress was reflected in my face as well. What Ray's look did tell me was this: We'll get through it. And I knew we would. And we did. But at a tremendous price, on many levels.

The worst had already passed. A month earlier, I had realized that despite our best business maneuvering, the battle was already lost. The bank had called in our loan to account for what had been the perfect storm of problems, one stemming from a unique idea: investing in Peacock Alley "boutiques." Quite common in retail now, these shops-within-shops were ahead of their time; ours were housed within 28 specialty stores and highlighted the products and style inspiration uniquely tailored to their consumers. And I still say had we had enough money in reserve and ample staffing, and had there not been a recession, we might have excelled. But, of course, we didn't, and the economy did nosedive, taking with it our best-laid plans—and my life savings.

Of everything I was losing, the most painful loss was $200,000 worth of stock I'd inherited from my mother after her death 12 years prior. It wasn't so much the dollar amount that hit me—it was that the stock had been such a source of strength for her—a woman who had spent most of her life capitulating to my father, and only later, after his passing, had found the strength to finally make decisions for herself. To buy the car she wanted, for instance. The money she'd inherited from her father, my grandfather, was her life's anchor, her backbone. By bolstering her self-respect, the stock had been her divine providence. Now it was mine, yet in a way I hadn't foreseen.

Thinking too deeply about all of this could have destroyed me, and Peacock Alley, so I had no choice but to give it up, to reach out for sup-

port from my family and move on. Deep down, I was at peace with that. Happiness, I've learned, comes from letting go. Money helps us do what makes us happy, of course, but it's not life's end-all, be-all. It can be replaced. Relationships and soul-fulfilling work can't.

Having hit bottom, I'd had nowhere to look—and go—but up. And through "the good times, bad times and goin' mad times," as Ray might say with his Texas charm, I've learned a great deal, all lessons I will share in these pages. Even truer to my mission will be to highlight life's real beauty: the positive people and comforting things we choose to have around us.

Throughout life's twists and turns, I've held close the blessings of family and friends, good food and health, fulfilling work, and life's unexpected moments of joy. But the common thread between them— what makes me feel happy, secure, warm and home, no matter where I am in this world—is something simple as this: beautiful textiles sewn with love and care. Pure, luxurious, homespun comfort.

I have two early, vivid memories to help explain this. And in each, I'm about three years old. (That was a long time ago, but I've done my best to paint an accurate picture of these anecdotes, based on my own memories and details told to me by others over the years.) In the first recollection, I'm with my mother and father at my maternal grandparents' farm in Jamestown, Pa., a tiny borough on the Shenango River in the western part of the state. A fall storm is brewing, with a strong wind blowing from the direction of Lake Erie. Snow is rising on the ground outside, making the temperature in the farmhouse fall. I can see it's dark outside and so I'm wearing a heavy flannel nightgown, one made by either my mother or my grandmother, who made most of my clothes back then.

In front of me is a bed that seems gigantic. Taking aim, I hitch up my

PAGE 017) Dotted Swiss
fabrics have always been
a favorite. We've used
it in past collections at
Peacock Alley, and these
curtains are in a bathroom
at my husband John's
family home in Martha's
Vineyard. A porcelain
pitcher holds wildflowers
gathered from the yard.
PAGE 018) My great
grandparents at the family
farm in Jamestown, Pa.
LEFT) Whenever possible,
I hang sheets on the line
to dry in the sunshine,
as they are here at the
farm in Granbury, Texas.

gown, put one foot on the side rail, and with all my might pull myself up
atop the mattress, resisting my mother's help but getting it anyway. Then,
flipping over after having landed face first, I slowly sink into the feathered
mattress. The muslin sheets are cold at first, but soon comes the unfurling
of my grandmother's winter quilts. Unlike the cotton, colorful patchwork
quilts of summer, these are wool, rustic, more bulky. The patterns are
larger, too, and the colors darker—gray, maroon, blue, even some black.
As I'm snug and warm, my mind drifts into sleep. To this day I remember
that moment as heaven on earth.

The next memory takes me to the old Dowling School House, a former
little red schoolhouse turned community center not far from my grandparents' home. It's a rather spartan place when empty, but for my grandmother's Country Sewing Club, beauty emanates from the center of the
room, where a large frame holds a quilt in progress. My grandmother and
six or seven friends gather there weekly to stitch and eat tureen dinners
and talk, most likely at that time about the town's young men fighting in

World War II. But oblivious to it all, I'm under the quilting frame in my own little world. Hearing their muffled voices, I guess who is who from the surrounding dress hems, shoes and stockings, and imagine the threads dangling from the quilts above as cobwebs in a cave. My cohorts-in-play are my Moreland cousins, as close to me as brothers and sisters. It's dark and cozy. I feel safe.

In the years that follow, safety and security would not always be ensured for me. But during the hardest times, I'd draw upon comforting childhood memories, or reach for one of the quilts my grandmother made with such care and love. Without fail, they have helped me get through.

I was named after both of my grandmothers—Marianna on my father's side (whom I never knew) and Ella on my mother's. Ella Beach Moreland and my grandfather, Charles Wilmot "C.W." Moreland, were better known to me as Grandma and Grandpappy.

AFTERNOONS WITH OLLIE

Freshly laundered sheets swaying on a line in the sunshine is more than a quaint visual for me. It's a sentimental reminder of my neighbor, Mrs. Ollie Foreman.

Each day after elementary school I'd present myself at the back steps of her house, and when the screen door opened, my afternoons with Ollie began. What we talked about I haven't a clue, but on each visit, the same routine unfolded. I'd help her take down the sheets she'd hand-washed earlier in the day and sit in her kitchen while she starched and ironed them to wrinkle-free perfection. Then I'd help her neatly fold them. This routine went on every day unless her arthritis was bothering her. All of this fascinated me, since in our house the washing was done only on Mondays, and it was a chore. For Ollie, it was sheer spiritual devotion. Life, she said, didn't get much better than being covered by the fresh smell of sunshine each evening.

At the first notion of spring, we'd take tours of her garden to check on her husband's peonies, watching the beautiful pale-pink bobbles slowly flower out like pom-poms. Her passion for seeing to the flowers' health in turn piqued my interest in my mother's favorite flower, lilacs, which I always cut and gave to Mother. What an incredible fragrance they have, especially when coated with morning dew.

Capping each of my visits with Ollie was tea time. We'd sip daintily from the demitasse cups of a Tiffany-blue Nippon porcelain china set graced with white swans. I was given that antique set by Ollie shortly before her death, and it means the world to me. I am eager to find replacements for the pieces that have broken over the years. And once a more respectable collection of china comes together, I'd love to share tea and conversation, Ollie-style, with my granddaughters.

Grandma Ella was a quiet, strong and churchgoing soul who expressed her love mostly with what she made and gave. I will say she was especially stern when it came to me. She took a disciplined approach to everything she did, be it sewing or crocheting, picking vegetables for canning, rendering lard and making soap, or washing clothes on a scrub board before hanging them out on a line to dry.

Grandpappy was a math and Latin teacher whose intellect and compassion were held in high esteem by not only his students but almost everyone who knew him. By the time I came along, he was beginning to spend more time farming, a chapter in his life captured in a cherished photo I have of him on the tractor, with me at age 2 sitting on his lap. As a learned man—a gentleman farmer, if you will—he would read to me constantly and help me with my school lessons. He was so kind, so patient and so confident I could learn anything and should learn everything. As educational amusement, he'd pull out one of his many books and take me on adventures of the imagination, making that farmhouse—and subsequent homes—a living storybook.

Around 1946, when I was 5, the bonds with my grandparents grew stronger when they moved from Jamestown to a small farm outside Chambersburg where we lived. From Grandpappy and others, I learned of the historic enclave's 18th- and 19th-century battles between the Iroquois, Lenape and Shawnee Native American tribes and our Appalachian Valley region's Scots-Irish settlers, in addition to our town's role in providing safe harbor for escaped slaves traveling the Underground Railroad. Because Chambersburg is only 13 miles north of Maryland—the Mason-Dixon Line—the town took a beating during the Civil War. It was set ablaze in 1864, making it the northernmost town burned by Confederates and inspiring the Union troops' rally cry "Remember Chambersburg!"

In my world, however, Chambersburg was an oasis of calm—an idyllic American place with a regal courthouse and towering fountain in its downtown square. Within the town two creeks intersect—the Conococheague (a Potomac tributary and noted trout stream) and Falling Spring. The area has a large farming population, including some Amish and a large number of Mennonite families, quiet people who almost seem to live two centuries behind, untouched by modern stresses. They live simply off the land, without electricity for daily-living needs and wearing dark colors as adults, and channel their creative spirits into sewing some of the most remarkable quilts on earth. They inspired the town's non-Mennonite ladies like my grandmother to show that they, too, could make beautiful quilts.

My grandparents' arrival in Chambersburg had a purpose that my young mind didn't comprehend. Though it was never discussed, I'm certain they moved to be closer to us after my mother and father discovered my 3-year-old brother, Robert Charles Butz, had leukemia. I was too young to truly understand what was happening. I just recall him crying in agonizing pain while my mother rocked him back and forth, talking softly to him to comfort him. And I remember most clearly being at the doctor's office when we all learned "Bobby" had only three months to live.

Those final days for him are a blur to me, since I wasn't really capable of grasping the headiness of it all. To cope, I withdrew more and more. After Bobby's death, I started spending more time with my grandparents, who included me in all of their farm tasks. I helped harvest corn, potatoes, beans, parsnips and tomatoes. I even helped pick peaches and apples, which Grandmother turned into sauces and jellies and baked into beautiful pies.

ABOVE) My mother Etta MacGregor Moreland.

RIGHT) My father Frank Daniel Butz.

OPPOSITE) My grandfather, Charles Wilmot "C.W." Moreland on a tractor with me at age 2, at our family farm in western Pennsylvania.

As my mother, Etta Moreland Butz, grieved over the loss of Bobby, she suffered what was at the time called a "nervous disorder." Now I realize it was a case of deep depression, which carried with it intense migraines that sent her to bed for days at a time. The stress for my father, Frank, resulted in a major stomach ulcer. Occasionally we'd drive south to get away from it all and have some "fun." Unfortunately, my parents' illnesses and fog of grief traveled with us, making it painfully quiet in that cavernous Buick. Then, as if life couldn't get any worse, I got the chickenpox while in Florida. Mother nursed me through it until I was well enough to return to Chambersburg. That's when I promptly came down with scarlet fever. I recall being relegated to my darkened bedroom for what seemed like an eternity, with my mother coming in often to offer food and comfort. What I remember most is the silence.

Looking back, the weight of such misfortune must have been too much for my parents to bear. I just wish I could talk now with my mother about it, to thank her for her strength, to talk with her about how she coped. She was always taking care of everyone but herself, and I wish I could have helped her more—to share her burden in some way. Back then, no one talked about their "feelings." We all learned to just tuck them away in a dark place somewhere. That left me painfully shy and quiet. So whenever I was home I either retreated to my room or was led out to play with cousins and friends.

Being outdoors was a real comfort. I spent as much time as possible playing tennis, golf and, of particular interest to my father, baseball. In his prime, Daddy played professional baseball for the Cincinnati Reds' farm team in Wheeling, W. Va., until an arm injury sidelined his dream. Though I'm sure he wished he could have been teaching Bobby baseball's finer points, I made a good substitute until my younger brother Franklin came along. Daddy successfully taught me how to pitch, hit and properly use a glove, making me good enough to play on our neighborhood's all-boys sandlot team. In the 1950s, such inclusion was uncommon, but back then I didn't know that. I felt their equal, and they treated me as such. I'm sure that helped give me the confidence I'd later need while working in a male-dominated business world.

My most girlish moments can be seen in old Easter photos, with me donning a store-bought outfit—usually a dress with matching coat and hat. (This was a rare treat, since mostly I had worn homemade clothing.) Daddy would give Mother and me a gardenia corsage that smelled so exotic. It made me feel as ladylike as my mother, whom I favored in appearance. We shared the same facial features and light, freckled complexion, but I wished for her red hair instead of my mousy brown. Also, in contrast to her curves, I was rail-thin from being so active in sports.

Providing balance to the outgoing, manly men on my father's side, Mother was a softer spirit, more like her courtly father. In step with her mother, she learned to sew, crochet and cook, and was a member in excellent standing of the Chambersburg Garden Club, where she learned the art of flower arranging. She wanted me to absorb all of these things, some of which, especially sewing, I did.

Mother also dressed impeccably in crisp suits, dresses and coats. It was important to Daddy that she do so—so much so that I remember him taking her shopping. As co-owner (with his brothers) of the town's Modern Home Appliance Co., he wanted to look the part of success and have her do likewise. Perhaps he got this trait from his Polish father, who, even when money was tight, made sure his and his sons' suits were tailor-made—a rarity in the coal-dusted, dirt-street town where they lived.

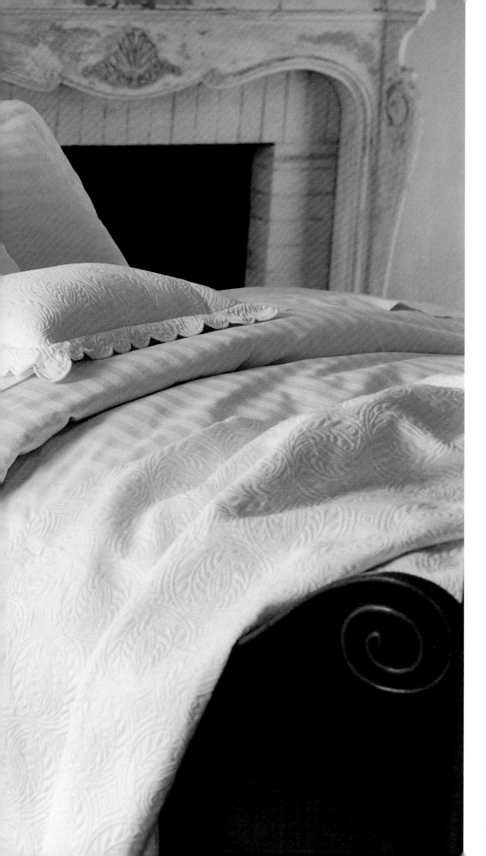

LEFT) Peacock Alley's
first matelassé bedding,
Vienna, debuted in 1999.

Favoring his father's looks, Daddy was very handsome, 6 feet 2 inches tall, dark-complected, with the chiseled features of a movie star and a public persona to match. At home, he also exhibited his father's controlling manner, with sky-high standards that could be a struggle to meet.

When Daddy was happy, he played the piano. He'd learned to play by ear as a child in his family's "band," which, along with pierogi-making, was always at the heart of our family's Polish-style celebrations. Mother had been formally trained on the piano, so her music was classic and soothing to the ear. And because I was expected to be formally trained, my music followed suit. Ours were the melodies that comforted Daddy when he'd come home for lunch, sit next to the fireplace near the piano, and unwind.

For my father, and most men at the time, women were expected to be the family caretakers, best suited for domesticity rather than business. But as I got older, and watched women disappear behind the scenes, I didn't see myself following in those footsteps.

OPPOSITE) This was taken at John's family home on Martha's Vineyard. The red and white quilt is typical of quilts made during the 1930s.

The one place Daddy and I did seem to connect as equals of sorts was on the golf course. That's when he'd loosen up and show a softer side, much as he had during my baseball training. It made him happy to teach me. To this day, every time I play golf I think of his advice: "Keep your head down, eye on the ball and follow through."

I wish the same discipline and drive had benefited me during my school years. I never embraced the strict rules of institutional learning, perhaps rebelling against the rigidity I faced at home. After elementary school, I attended the all-girls Penn Hall Preparatory School. (In our Mennonite community, girls weren't educated after age 15 or 16, so public education was lacking.) Then I headed to Washington, D.C., to study physical education at Marjorie Webster Junior College. It was there, away from my father's watchful eye, that I saw my chance to fully embrace life, which seemed much more interesting than a stack of textbooks.

Conspiring against studiousness was my "dorm," which for 40 of us that year was an all-women's hotel halfway between the school and downtown Washington. This location was not a smart choice on the school's part, I must say; the bright lights and big capital city were too much of a magnet. I also must've thought I was on vacation, since each week I'd send home my dirty clothes in a large metal trunk via Greyhound Bus. Like magic, the trunk would reappear the following week from Chambersburg, with everything inside it beautifully cleaned and ironed by my saintly mother.

One college did garner my interest, but not for higher learning: the University of Virginia in Charlottesville. Its parties were legendary, as I can attest. One night I even played a game of pool in a fraternity house with "Great Balls of Fire" singer Jerry Lee Lewis, who was in town to entertain. (Side note: Billiards was yet another sport that I liked, enough so that the owner of Chambersburg's pool hall was certain I could have a career in it. He even tried to talk me into meeting a rep from Brunswick. Upon learning this, my parents—who had no idea I'd ever even dream of being in that pool hall, much less be one of its top players—were mortified. And that, as they say, was that.)

After a year at Marjorie Webster, I realized that even if I buckled down with my books, the only career I could have in physical education was teaching it, which wasn't appealing. So, at age 21, I headed back to Chambersburg to work for my father and figure out Plan B.

During my nine months there I saw with fresh perspective "the Butz way" of doing business, which at its core was a tremendously strong work ethic gleaned from my Polish grandparents. The Butz brothers—my father Frank and his brothers Joe, Stan and John—were forward-thinking businesspeople who started their business in 1936 with only one Maytag washing machine, which, after being sold, paid for two more to sell, which paid for four more, etc. There was never a doubt the brothers wouldn't be successful. If they had a good day, great. If they had a bad day, well, everyone just needed to work harder. Simple as that. What's more, it would never have occurred to them that they could have done other things with their lives. They saw working together as a blessing. And it was.

There was another important dynamic I witnessed and have tried to encourage in my own family business: never a harsh word spoken between family members. All were extremely protective of each other, and that love and respect strengthened their desire to succeed. That mind-set carried over to the four brothers' three sisters, too. If one's husband wasn't doing well financially, they got together to help him out. There was no discussion about it. That's just what families did.

My father and uncles also were astute enough to allow people to buy on credit and layaway, which many businesses didn't do in those days. But it was the dark side of that privilege—working in collections—that turned me off. While going with Daddy and the sheriff to collect a lady's washing machine—carting it off as she rode atop it, pleading and crying—I was appalled. Witnessing this display, and knowing there'd be many more like it, simply confirmed that such work wasn't for me. By my early 20s I was ready to lead a more interesting life, one that very easily could have popped from the pages of my grandfather's books about daring people in dreamy locations. And I had the perfect plan, one I'd hatched with a couple of friends from my Marjorie Webster days: I would be a flight attendant.

In the early 1960s, being a stewardess was considered one of the most glamorous occupations a girl could have. My friend Robin Mossman, her roommate Gayle Gunderman and I had it in our heads to take the world by storm—well, airplane—and be based in New York City. We filled out our applications with Pittsburgh-based Allegheny Airlines. There was

a problem, however, that Butz determination and Moreland creativity wouldn't help. I didn't meet Allegheny's physical requirements. I was too skinny. They didn't want Twiggy; they wanted more, say, Natalie Wood. I was crushed. But not for long. Robin and Gayle had landed jobs with the airline and wanted a roommate to share their New Jersey apartment.

With little prompting, and half-hearted support from my family, I was on the next train north with $40 in my wallet and, of course, my golf clubs (just what a struggling girl would need in the city!). Nonetheless, my Butz-Moreland genes, paired with a competitive streak picked up from playing sports, had officially kicked in. I didn't know where I ultimately was headed, but when I saw the New York City skyline, I was fearless.

AN IRISH WEAVER'S YARN

One of my ancestors was Irish weaver Isaac Moreland, son of Scottish weavers John and Letitia Moreland. Their cottage and weaver shop stood on the banks of the River Bann, an important route in the industrialization of northern Ireland's linen industry. After learning the craft from his family, Isaac served for several years as an apprentice to a Scottish weaver, and by age 21 he had saved enough money to, along with his 18-year-old brother William (my grandfather's father) seek a more profitable life in the newly established United States of America.

In 1793 the brothers set sail for Philadelphia on the British schooner "Little Mary." Isaac and William worked whatever jobs they could to save enough to buy inexpensive land in the sparsely populated western part of the state. Family records show the duo acquired 850 acres from the 20-year-old U.S. government for a grand total of $2,000. Then in 1796, Isaac and William headed west and became some of the first settlers in what would become Westmoreland County (named for their family). As our family lore has it, Isaac built a sturdy house with stone quarried by the Moreland brothers near Jamestown around 1819. For at least a century the homestead remained in the family, and an old photo of mine (opposite page), shows a spinning wheel next to the fireplace with iron cooking pots. My grandfather C.W. Moreland is pictured below as a young man.

POLISH PIONEERS

My father's father, Sam Butz, lived out most of his life in Greenwald, a tiny coal-company town at the foothills of Pennsylvania's Allegheny Mountains not far from Pittsburgh. The rolling, heavily forested region must have felt familiar to him in a way, since his early life was spent in the Tatra Mountains of southern Poland, also the home of his future wife, Marianna Bunda. In 1878, "Sebastian Budz," as he was known before the last name's misspelling in America, was born in a land being fought over by Austria, Russia and Prussia. The resulting no-man's-land of farmers had become impoverished, prompting young men and women (including Sam's sister) to leave for opportunities in booming, Industrial Age America.

At 18, Sam faced two choices: Join the Austrian army and face almost certain death in Russia for a cause he knew really nothing about, or join his sister in Pennsylvania, where coal-mining jobs were plentiful. He chose freedom. But the path to America wouldn't be easy.

Traveling on foot, mostly at night to escape capture by the Austrian army, Sam traversed some 500 miles to Hamburg's North Sea port. There he worked odd jobs until he'd earned enough to travel on the steamship in steerage, a journey across the Atlantic that took about a month, "confined shoulder-to-shoulder with hundreds of other emigrants in the squalid lower deck of an oceangoing purgatory," as my cousin Dick Butz relates in *Back Home.* "He never spoke of the steamy, airless quarters; the ceaseless clanking and pounding of the giant engines just beneath them, of the stench, the illness, the anxiety and confusion. Perhaps all that was forgotten with his first breath of fresh air and first glimpse of Lady Liberty in the New York City harbor." Remarkably, the statue had been there only a decade at the time.

Sam didn't speak a word of English, but a network of Polish emigrants helped him reunite with his sibling in Crabtree, where he eventually found work in the coal mines. His betrothed, Marianna, joined him with money loaned by her parents, and they were married by a Polish priest in 1902. They had eight children including my father Frank. By 1909 work was sound enough for the family to move from a small shack to a two-room cabin in Greenwald. While Sam worked in the mines, Marianna tended to domestic duties, including one that gives me chills to think about. To obtain water from a creek that ran alongside an electrified railroad line, my grandmother would carry it, two buckets at a time, three or four times a day, about a quarter of a mile each way on a very narrow trail next to the tracks. That meant on cold and wet days, which were often, if her skirt touched the third rail, which it often did, she'd get an electrical shock. (That certainly puts our own trivialities in perspective.)

When the mines closed in the region in the early 1920s, and real estate was left vacant and sold for pennies on the dollar, Sam wisely snapped up the property to rent and re-sell in better times. He also recognized that without a mine, there was no company store, and a town needed a store to survive. With his money tied up in property, my grandmother turned to her brother for help. In exchange for cash, she traded to Frank Bunda her portion of family land in Poland. And with that, The Butz General Store came to be. For more than a decade, the store served double duty as Greenwald's go-to spot for everything from canned goods to hardware to gas, as well as a community meeting place where men played cards and people made calls from the only phone in town. Each Easter it even served as a makeshift chapel of sorts, where, on Holy Saturday, a priest would be on hand to bless the townspeople's baskets of homemade fare—breads, jams, cheese, fancy Easter eggs—covered in each family's finest hand-embroidered cloth.

Uncle Joe's Old Fashioned

INGREDIENTS
Simple Syrup
Candied Oranges and Lemons
Maraschino Cherries
Bitters
VO
Club Soda
Ice

DIRECTIONS
Muddle oranges, lemon, cherry and a couple
drops of bitters together, add 2-3 teaspoons
of simple syrup in an old fashioned glass, fill
the glass with ice, pour VO
add a splash of club soda

UNCLE JOE'S OLD FASHIONED

My uncle Joe made a cocktail that became legendary in our family—one we call Uncle Joe's Old Fashioned. We had them at every family gathering and special occasion. "Daddy always said, 'We're only going to have one, but it's going to be a good one!'" my first cousin Susan Dugan said of her father's famous drink. "Sometimes we had two!" I still serve Uncle Joe's special cocktail whenever family gathers.

2 to 3 teaspoons simple syrup (see Notes)
2 dashes bitters
2 slices lemon
1 orange slice, quartered
2 maraschino cherries (one reserved for garnish)
2 ounces blended Canadian whisky (see Notes)
Splash of club soda

In an old fashioned glass, combine the simple syrup, bitters, lemon and orange slices, and one cherry. Muddle well to combine. Fill glass with ice cubes. Add blended whisky and stir. Top with splash of club soda and garnish with remaining cherry. Notes: To make simple syrup, stir to 1/2 cup granulated sugar with 1/2 cup water, and bring to a boil; remove from heat once sugar is completely dissolved; let cool before using. Uncle Joe liked Seagram's V.O.

Makes 1 cocktail.

2 RISK

You gain strength, courage and confidence by every experience in which you really stop to look fear in the face.

—ELEANOR ROOSEVELT

Our first apartment was near the Newark, N.J., airport. It may have been convenient for Robin and Gayle, who by now had their Allegheny Air stewardess wings, but we soon realized that the stark place was nowheresville for three single women eager to embrace life across the Hudson River. After an exhaustive search, we settled on a one-bedroom apartment in what was one of New York City's most affordable neighborhoods in 1961, Greenwich Village.

Little did we know how interesting our new world would be. Located on Perry Street between Bleeker and Houston, our place was tiny. But during the week when Robin and Gayle were flying, I had it to myself and life was pretty cozy. Outside, however, I was definitely out of my comfort zone. For starters, I was rather preppy. Greenwich Village was not. Bob Dylan had just arrived to join the thriving folk scene, which was blending in with the writer-poet beatniks who'd earlier claimed many of the neighborhood's smoky bars. Free-spirited musicians played bongos and artists sold their paintings in Washington Square, while in coffeehouses, discussions focused on the mind and spirituality. And on the streets I learned to walk at a clipped pace that was faster than most people in Chambersburg would even think to move, even in a hurry.

Life slowed considerably at our neighborhood haunt, Marie's Crisis Cafe. The basement bar was as dark as tar until our eyes could adjust to it, and Marie herself played the piano while encouraging sing-alongs. The bar was in a house where during the Revolutionary War Thomas Paine had written his philosophical series "The American Crisis." A century later the place had been a brothel. By the time we were enjoying it, the establishment had taken on a rebellious and jolly patina. Every type of restaurant surrounded us but we never had the money to visit one unless someone else was buying. We also were so busy doing whatever it was we

PAGE 048) This floral centerpiece, pictured at our loft in Fort Worth, was done by our dear friend Joe Don Watts. The Spode china with its simple gold band was my wedding china and the crystal goblets were my mother's. **RIGHT)** My engagement picture, 1966. **BELOW)** Marie's Crisis Cafe, our hangout in Greenwich Village in New York City during the 1960s.

were doing that we'd often forget to eat, or wind up nibbling on street food. I don't think we even once cooked a meal. As proof: We unplugged our refrigerator to use it for sweater storage!

It was during my Penn Hall senior excursion to Bermuda that I met my first crush. Dale was from Bronxville, just north of Manhattan, and his knowledge of the Big Apple and its arts scene was impressive. Plus, he was quite literally tall, dark and handsome—in addition to being smart—which for me was the ultimate combination. Our Manhattan cultural outings were fun, but the long-distance relationship didn't survive. What did survive was my desire to one day know the city as well as Dale had. And, even more so, make it mine.

When a Manhattan employment agency informed me I could type only 28 words a minute, I wasn't deterred. If there was a job out there, I could learn to do it. That's just what happened after I answered a newspaper ad from a small and successful public relations firm looking for a receptionist. But looking back, this career chapter could definitely have been an episode for the AMC series "Mad Men." My job was to assist two men who handled some of the world's top luxury accounts. Before I knew it I was attending glamorous parties on yachts where Champagne flowed freely and diamonds and sequins sparkled. I was out of my league in the social stratosphere, but somehow made it through.

For support I found myself leaning on one of the firm's principals. He had captivated me with his wit, charming way with clients and creative writing ability. His positive response to my work, primarily crafting press releases and arranging appointments, made me feel that for the first time in my life I had something of value to contribute. (What a revelation to a shy girl raised in a family that didn't communicate a lot.) I believe now that I needed such encouragement from someone like him, especially since my father, the only successful man I'd worked with until then, hadn't taken my work seriously.

Normally a man 20 years my senior, one newly separated from his wife, wouldn't have appealed to me. But the more he helped me, the more I grew, both professionally and personally. We eventually dated, but jealousy on his part ended our relationship quite dramatically. One evening, after returning home from a night of partying with friends, I found him waiting for me in my apartment, holding a butcher knife and seething. I was beyond stunned, as I had given him no encouragement that ours was a serious relationship. After seeing I wasn't with a male rival, he flung the knife to the kitchen floor—where it lodged vertically—and angrily walked out. He had scared us both; I could see it in his face. I also could see it was time to move on.

My confidence was shaken with my first real love, John Dunlop. That's when I came face-to-face with cold, hard elitism. John and I had met at a party in the Village, and afterward were inseparable. I really thought he was "the one." But when he left the city to get his MBA at an Ivy League school, our relationship changed for the worse. That's when I got to know his family. During weekend trips to see him, I'd stay with his brother, a professor, and his wife, both of whom told me in so many words that I wasn't their family's cup of tea.

For them, and John's parents, academics was everything. For the first time in my life I was assessed to be, at least in the family's minds, a nobody. I'd gone to private girls' schools, yes, but not to one of the "right" schools. I could see they'd assessed me as being nothing more than a dalliance. My bruised ego, combined with our long-distance romance, unraveled the relationship. Though my personal life was suffering, the experience intensified my commitment and desire to succeed professionally.

During this difficult time, I found a much-needed distraction in working for a sophisticated public relations firm run by Mabel Flanley and Sally Woodward. Both had risen to prominence after being selected by President Franklin Roosevelt to help lead the War Production Board, which encouraged women to help conserve materials and fuel during World War II. By 1944 the duo had been successful enough to open their own Midtown Manhattan firm, with the motto "The Women's Angle in Public Relations."

Mabel, a statuesque woman who reminded me of Eleanor Roosevelt, had a stately presence, and she was the driving force of the business. Sally, more slight in build and demeanor, carried out most of the creative duties. From the periphery, I paid close attention to how they handled their accounts—which were mostly home and lifestyle—for such companies

CLASSICALLY TRAINED

As a young woman, I emulated the best-dressed woman I knew: my mother, Etta Moreland Butz. But I did so in my own generation's way, of course.

Dressing simply wasn't difficult to do in the 1950s and early 1960s, when prim sweaters and skirts, pearls and pumps were de rigueur. By the mid-1960s, however, when everything went mod and mini, I didn't blindly follow the trends, like many I knew. I decided to keep my style simple and classic. Audrey Hepburn and Jackie Kennedy were my style compasses. They stuck to the basics, from hair styles to shoes, and looked chic through the decades despite the fashion fads swirling around them. Early on in life I'd learned from my mother and father that if you invested in well-made clothing, and cared for it properly, it would last for years and always look "in."

Following that credo, I kept a mix of gray, light brown, dark brown, navy, white and beige clothing. And, of course, the ubiquitous black dress. Using that scheme I then chose durable yet luxe textures—soft cashmeres, boucle wool, striated linen and crisp cotton. I could accent the outfits, simply but in a stand-out way, with accessories including well-made leather shoes and handbags, and then a silk scarf for color pattern or a strand of pearls for a more streamlined look. For dressier occasions I added my mother's pearl brooch (pictured opposite) or a dressy watch; for even finer occasions I might wear my black dress with a sleek rhinestone necklace and maybe just a simple circle pin, and tuck a satin clutch under my arm.

In retrospect, my classic take on style still contributes to the mind-set for my textile business. We've created all of Peacock Alley's lines around the little black dress theory: Own the best basics and thoughtfully work everything else in. Our emphasis on timelessness continually sets us apart from the competition.

as Purex, the California Prune Advisory Board and Washington State's Processed Apples Board. Beyond my clerical duties, my most visible role was serving them tea every afternoon, when they'd come together in an elegant sitting room between their offices to discuss the state of their accounts. It was all so dignified. I rather liked the graciousness of it all and decided I wanted such a life.

In a 1955 issue of Public Relations Journal, Mabel and Sally divulged what they believed every female public relations professional should be: well-versed in a wide range of public relations activities; knowledgeable of women's issues and the top female opinion leaders; skilled in business and, particularly, in working well with management; and immensely respectful of her employer. Such qualities were ones I set out to master during my time working for them.

In proving I had a strong work ethic and could meet deadlines while juggling a load of clerical duties, I won the respect of Flanley and Woodward's production manager, who hired me as her assistant. I received a slight raise from my $400-per-month salary, which had been just enough to keep my nose above water. By now I felt like I was getting somewhere. But while listening to Mabel and Sally converse with clients about the complex issues of the day—President Kennedy's assassination or civil rights legislation—I realized that part of me needed bolstering. Hungry to learn, and wanting to make a good impression, I began buying the daily newspapers as well as *Time* magazine.

Only a few years before, the idea of working with successful women had been foreign to me, based on how my father's business was run. In that world, women weren't expected to carry on enlightened conversations. But for me, that would change. As would my style sensibilities. I'd grown up knowing the niceties of life, surrounded at home by the very latest furnishings from my family's store, but when I was invited to a party at Mabel's apartment in Murray Hill, I was in awe. Her tastes were different from anything I'd known. Exotic, even. Her mix of collected art and antiques, complemented by modern furnishings, opened my eyes to a way of living that was as chic as I wanted to be.

In 1963 I would meet, briefly date and eventually work with a man who later became a feared corporate raider and, according to a 2011 article in *Forbes*, an inspiration for the fictional Gordon Gekko character of the Wall Street movies. At the time, however, all I knew was that Asher Edelman was a young lion on the financial scene—and the epitome of cool.

Asher was living with Marty Gordon, an up-and-coming art dealer whom my roommate Gayle had begun dating. We meshed beautifully, and all of us fell in together like we'd known each other for ages. And what wasn't to like about two handsome, charismatic guys living in a beautiful Greenwich Village townhouse full of modern art with an Aston Martin parked outside?

Asher had been working as an assistant manager at Halle & Stieglitz, a stock brokerage house known as "an old firm with young ideas." Asher was driving those "young ideas" and I was swept up in his dynamism. He offered me a job assisting him, which I readily accepted. Flanley and Woodward had been nice and stable, but this career move could offer the opportunity to work in a highly energetic environment. Asher and I hadn't worked together long before he was tapped by a newly formed brokerage firm, Carter, Berlind and Weill, as head of its options and arbitrage division. So off I followed, keen to learn everything I could about Asher's world.

The buying and selling of stocks and options was not something my

family was high on; they'd recently taken a bath in worthless Studebaker stock after the car company's nosedive. But I could see how stock investments could work with good research, salesmanship and instincts. Options trading was all about taking risks and being decisive. Asher and his partner, Bob Bushnell, encouraged me to learn the ropes in order to help with some of their accounts and ultimately bring in some of my own, which I did.

To watch Asher work, though, was to witness a force of nature. His grasp of the securities business was growing by the day, and he would go on to be a major player in the financial world. Asher's corporate raiding during the 1980s would be included in the 1990s *New York Times* bestseller *Barbarians at the Gate,* about the leveraged buyout of RJR Nabisco.

As for me, the upside of working on Wall Street was managing to not let the old boys' club atmosphere stop me from trying to make a name for myself. As I'd done as a girl trying to pitch better than the boys in

Chambersburg, I just decided I needed to work triply hard to keep up with, and even outpace, my teammates. Ultimately I proved that I could do just that, particularly when it came to my work with stock options in the growing airline sector. I also had done something truly significant: become a registered representative. For a female in 1965, that was almost unheard of. One of my greatest achievements, however, was seeing my father's look of surprise when I told him he'd made a significant return on an investment I'd suggested. That felt good. Meanwhile money was coming in from the sideline quilt-trading business Gayle and I were enjoying. At this point in life I realized I was no longer out of my league, but rather a respected player.

OPPOSITE) Peacock Alley's
Vienna matelassé shams.

LEFT) I purchased this chrome bar cart in one of our Peacock Alley stores for our loft in Fort Worth. It holds my collection of antique silver and crystal decanters— I love how it glitters when the sunlight streams through the windows.

TAKING STOCK

In 1965, my bosses, the soon-to-be-powerhouses Asher Edelman and Bob Bush-nell, said they wanted me to help them with their accounts. Fine. But the best way to do that was to take a course given by the New York Institute of Finance to prepare for and take the Series 7 General Securities Registered Represen-tative exam administered by the Financial Industry Regulatory Authority. Gulp.

At first I was a bit scared by the challenge. Me, a registered broker? Math has never been my strong suit, but in the case of brokerage work I did find it understandable and at times even enjoyable. Plus, my work in public relations and involvement in competitive sports had prepared me for the fast-paced world of Wall Street. I just wanted to do a better job for Asher and Bob—and also make the extra money they said would be possible by helping them.

Little did I know how unusual it was at that time for a woman to take the exam. I knew in our small firm the few females were assistants, as I was. But I also assumed that by this time there must be female stockbrokers, or Asher and Bob wouldn't have put me up to it. (Forward thinking they certainly were.) I studied rigorously (finding outstanding "tutors" at work) and, to my great relief, passed the test.

I felt special for a number of reasons—mainly for overcoming my fear of the test. Only later, when I heard all of the publicity about Muriel Siebert, did I realize what a breakthrough my effort truly was. On December 28, 1967, Siebert became the first woman to not only own a seat on the New York Stock Exchange, but also head one of its member firms. Early on, though, she had battled ridicule and harassment, which she chronicles in her book, *Changing the Rules: Adventures of a Wall Street Maverick* (Simon and Schuster, 2002).

Now known as "the First Woman of Finance," Siebert has said, "The men at the top of industry and government should be more willing to risk sharing leadership with women and minority members who are not merely clones of their white male buddies. In these fast-changing times we need the different viewpoints and experiences, we need the enlarged talent bank. The real risk lies in continuing to do things the way they've always been done."

I was bucking the system, and it went hand-in-hand with me being the only girl on the all-boys baseball team in Chambersburg, Pa., and one of the few women who played golf or pool. It just goes to show how, with the right encouragement, motivation and training—and a healthy dose of naïveté— anyone can accomplish what others believe impossible.

LEFT) The New York Stock Exchange

3 DRIVEN

To love what you do and feel that it matters—
how could anything be more fun?

—KATHARINE GRAHAM

PAGE 068) My grandmother made this pale green and white quilt, which is done in a classic Amish pattern from the 1930s.

OPPOSITE) These antique quilts, done in classic Double Wedding Ring and Grandmother's Flower Garden patterns, were some of the original ones Gayle and I purchased when we started our quilt trading business in New York City.

I'm quite certain I was the only Wall Street professional dealing in the commodity of fine, old quilts. It was a pastime Gayle and I enjoyed—buying, selling and trading them. We never made much profit—we kept "trading up" for rarer ones. But each "find" often had an interesting story, which for us made it priceless.

With pop art in full swing in the mid-1960s, patchwork bedding was so uncool that it was cool. Our Pennsylvania Dutch-country backgrounds gave us a unique advantage, and we had access to many of the country's finest quilts, which we began to see as true American art forms.

Extra money I made from brokerage commissions often went into acquiring quilts, but increasingly it was invested in more traditional art, such as 19th-century drawings and lithographs. With art everywhere in New York, and gallery openings regular forms of entertainment for us, I began to recognize how much I favored the simple and classic drawings and the bold designs of Cubism. I now see how lines and patterns, in textiles and on paper or canvas, ultimately inspired my life's work and passion: linens for the home. That would come to fruition within a decade, but before then I had other adventures to experience.

One originated on a Sunday afternoon while I was out-and-about in the city with friends. A showroom of shiny Honda motor scooters caught our attention, so we popped inside for a closer look. None of us had any intention of buying one. But it was there I'd fall under the spell of one of the most persuasive men I'd ever meet—Michael Needleman—and leave the showroom the owner of my very own Honda 50.

The attraction between us was instant. Michael was as good-looking as he was charming, but what's more, he had an impressive work ethic. Moonlighting at the Honda dealership was his weekend job; his primary work was as a sales manager for F.B. Rogers Silver Co.

Michael offered to teach me to drive the scooter in city traffic, which I happily allowed him to do. Afterward we began spending almost all of our free time together, trying new ethnic restaurants, riding horseback in Central Park or motorcycling to Fire Island. He was always on the go and aimed high, having been raised by a driven family in Forest Hills, Long Island, before earning a business degree at the University of Maine.

When we decided to marry, I met his family and he met mine. I was nervous about his visit to Chambersburg. My Protestant parents had been grappling with why I would want to marry someone Jewish, and why I would need to convert to Judaism to do so. But after meeting Michael they never again questioned my decision. They were as wowed by him as I was.

For a time, life was zipping along nicely until Michael learned that F.B. Rogers was transferring him to Dallas, effective immediately. Soon afterward, my parents became gravely ill (my father from a heart attack and stroke, my mother from a bleeding ulcer) and it was imperative that I leave New York for Chambersburg to help them.

In the span of a few months, life as I knew it had turned upside down. My family seemed to be slipping away. My wedding plans had been shelved. I had by then converted to a new religion. And soon I would be moving to Dallas, which seemed like the end of the earth. But through it all I focused only on my family, and fortunately my parents pulled through. Only then could I find the peace of mind I needed to pack up and head south.

When my plane touched down at Dallas' Love Field, so much I held dear was 1,500 miles behind me. However, I took comfort anticipating that a beautiful new world was ahead of me. On October 29, 1966, Michael and I were married in a rabbi's study at Temple Emanu-El. The intimate occasion was far from the chic event I'd planned for New York City's Lotos Club, but it was sweet in its simplicity. I wore the ivory peau de soie jacketed dress and short matching veil I'd bought at Bergdorf Goodman. And in subtle tribute to my mother and grandmother, I carried a small mix of roses and lilacs.

Michael and I headed to Acapulco to honeymoon at Las Brisas, a glitzy resort frequented by Liz and Dick, Elvis and others. In a setting nestled in a steep hillside of lush hibiscus gardens and palm trees, with a private pink and white casita facing Acapulco Bay's sumptuous sunsets, we drank in the stellar views from our perch, explored the city below and enjoyed a day of deep-sea fishing in the Pacific. Both of us were glowing—from the sun, Champagne and love. To say I was on top of the world was an understatement. Michael and I toasted to life together as well as our careers, which held so much promise. Well, at least for Michael. For me, landing a fulfilling job in Dallas would be much more challenging.

In mid-1960s Manhattan, professional women were the norm. In Dallas, they were the exception. Statistically, only one in five U.S. women with children under age 6 held paying jobs—and their earnings were still only 60 percent of men's, despite the Equal Pay Act of 1963. In Texas, women's rights would definitely take longer to arrive and ultimately to find acceptance. It wasn't until 1967 that a married woman could legally even have control of her earnings; before then her husband had to manage them. What's more, if someone wanted to hire a married woman, state law held that the employer technically needed permission from her husband.

I knew nothing of this. All I knew was that I'd just left a thriving career on Wall Street, where I'd worked with the financial world's rising stars and had broken new ground myself. I was certain a job with a Dallas brokerage firm would be quick in coming, and I'd also have an edge over any competition. After all, Dallas was like a sleepy satellite office compared to Wall Street.

I laugh thinking about it now, but what a shock it must have been for Dallas' old-boy stockbroker network to be approached by a 25-year-old woman wanting to join their team. Most women in Dallas worked as secretaries, teachers or sales clerks—certainly not registered brokers. "We'll take your interest under consideration," was their nonplussed response.

I also smile when I recall another temporary setback. Dallas women at the time wouldn't dare be seen riding a motor scooter in public, and my doing so raised many an eyebrow. (Four decades later, of course, it's a hip thing to do.) But in the end, selling my Honda 50 was probably for the best: There were so many potholes in the roads that riding it was bumpy, to say the least.

Beyond those proverbial and literal bumps in the road, I found Dallas delightful. Even in late fall, people were still cruising in open convertibles, dining on patios and lounging by pools in the warm sunshine. What's more, my taste buds had been forever captivated by Tex-Mex food.

I even began cooking, preparing such dishes as Pennsylvania Dutch chicken corn chowder and Grandma's apple pie, family recipes handwritten on index cards by my mother when I married and contained in a little box. How funny to picture those days, when portly Lancer's and Mateus wine bottles with drippy candles made cozy centerpieces in front of such dishes as beef stroganoff and chicken à la king (which indeed looked best in dim lighting).

While wanting to be hospitable and, hopefully, accepted, I studied Southerners' unceasing charm. Were they really so cheerful and polite all the time? Or was that just an affectation? Having spent most of my life around people who were reserved, even guarded, upon meeting someone new, I discovered Southerners to be truly sincere in their warmth. Everyone eagerly wanted to help me to get acclimated as soon as possible.

With the encouragement of one of my first new friends, I applied for a holiday job at Neiman Marcus, where, as *Time* magazine once noted, "all good millionaires outfitted their wives." To my surprise I was instantly

LEFT) This is one of my favorite spots to read when I'm at our house on Martha's Vineyard. The 1930s quilt over the back of the Adirondack chair belonged to John's family.

hired. And though my seasonal work lasted only two months, the experience was invaluable. It not only helped me to develop more sophisticated fashion sensibilities, it also led to some important, lifelong friendships. One in particular led to the creation of Peacock Alley—but more on that soon.

The main thing I realized during my short time at Neiman Marcus was how much I enjoyed selling. I'd grown up around strong salespeople, worked in public relations, and encouraged people to buy stocks and options. But I had never really applied myself in a retail setting. I now understood why so many in my family found it fulfilling. I, too, found great satisfaction interacting with people, meeting their needs and, even better, seeing them return for my help.

After my Neiman Marcus job ended, I was determined to join a brokerage firm, which, despite the odds, I managed to do. But unlike the dynamic job I'd had on Wall Street, at this particular Dallas firm I worked strictly as a secretary. That left me feeling uninspired, invisible even. I did wind up getting some responsibility when one of the firm's brokers realized I could fill in for him. But while I was proud of the work I did, all of it was kept under the radar, which wasn't where I wanted it to be. I moved on to a much larger firm, Smith Barney, where I handled my own accounts and could finally show what I could accomplish. But in 1969 my priorities changed with the birth of my first son, Jason. I'd be needed for one of the most important jobs in my life—being a mother.

During my early days in Dallas I remained in touch with my close friend and former roommate Gayle. Her firstborn child, a daughter, was born the same year as Jason, and with that, our bond grew even stronger. We talked at length by telephone about our children, sharing stories and offering advice. We also discussed our futures. Both of us loved motherhood, but we also needed a challenge. We not only wanted to think creatively, as we'd done during our quilt buying/trading collaboration, but to be worth more than just what our husbands provided for us.

The perfect opportunity arose when Gayle spotted a sweet little boudoir pillow with a patchwork quilt design in an upscale Madison Avenue boutique. How clever, she thought. We discussed it over the phone, and our imaginations were stoked.

Though I'd had only one semester of home economics in prep school, I was comfortable enough around sewing machines, having helped my mother with her projects and accomplishing my own, mostly simple ones. Gayle's skill level was similar to mine. So, we started out as two neophytes. But we were determined to make our own versions of those pillows, in this case by piecing together various floral and gingham fabric pieces to create pillows framed by white eyelet ruffles.

As hoped, they were hits with our friends, who'd received them as holiday gifts. But the true test would be whether we could sell them to stylish boutiques. Thankfully, the stores' savvy owners were equally enthused. Orders began rolling in. We knew we were on to something.

I found it immensely rewarding to not only be able to stay home and look after Jason, but also combine my sales skills and my creative abilities. Much like the ever-present patchwork fabrics—by then spilling out of every drawer and closet—my work interests seemed to be coming together nicely. (Well, at least from my perspective: What Michael sometimes saw as a reversal, I saw as progress.)

In 1971 my life would forever change thanks to an almost fairy tale event, one complete with an actual prince and princess. One evening, Michael and I hosted a dinner party that included Robert Leitstein, merchandise manager for Neiman Marcus. Noticing my handmade pillows, and their floral fabric accents, he was captivated. By the meal's end, he was convinced they'd be perfect for the store's upcoming Fortnight, an annual promotion of fashions and culture from a different country each year. The two-week extravaganza, which Stanley Marcus launched in 1957, drew worldwide dignitaries, celebrities and social elite, and it was magical—*Time* magazine dubbed it "Dallas in Wonderland." That year's event was a floral-themed promotion, Fête des Fleurs, which for the first time wasn't aligned with a particular region at all, but celebrated the beauty of flowers and flower-themed merchandise. It was a breakout idea that would prove to be an aesthetic and financial success for the retailer.

Within a day or so, Robert called to place the order. He'd need 250 pillows. In about a month. Gayle and I were thrilled—we'd made it to the big leagues almost overnight. But then, as we sewed pillows fast and furiously, night and day, both reality and delirium set in. We needed help or we'd never be able to deliver the pillows on time. I took out newspaper ads looking for seamstress help, which is how I met the amazing Sylvia Guerrero. She and I instantly clicked, and we ultimately worked together for four decades. But even Sylvia's fast work wasn't putting a dent in the order. Thankfully, and most unexpectedly, fate intervened.

Sadly and suddenly Michael's father died, which added even more strain to our situation. We hurriedly packed for Long Island, and I tried to keep my stress level in check, all the while knowing the Neiman Marcus order was pressing. My worries must have been apparent as I found myself seeking advice from a complete stranger seated next to me at a dinner after the funeral. The gentleman told me he owned a raincoat

BELOW) Here I am with Gayle
Gunderman, my roommate
and future partner in Peacock
Alley, at a market party in
New York City.

Fête des Fleurs

An Exposition of Flowers and Fashion

Neiman-Marcus/Dallas Texas/October 11-23

manufacturing business in New York City, and I told him about my order-fulfillment crisis. In turn he told me about a custom sewing business he ran on the side. "Why don't you send me a sample of the pillow," he offered. "I'll see if I can't get it produced for you." Like my guardian angel, he did just that. With his help, we got those pillows completed on time. (And I learned a valuable lesson: You can't do everything yourself. You have to partner to achieve your goals.)

During the store's Fortnight promotion, our pillows looked lovely in various displays, where the guests of honor, Monaco's Princess Grace and Prince Rainier, mingled with all of Dallas' beautiful people. It was thrilling. We'd been afforded unbelievable entrée into the highest strata of the retail world. Neiman Marcus was the trendsetter others tried to imitate. If you could make it there, well … you know the rest.

Looking back, my very first business crisis had been averted, if only through sheer serendipity. I had no way of knowing then how much that

OPPOSITE) Shams from
our quilted and hem-stitched
bedding ensembles.

early predicament would set the stage for Peacock Alley's future. Many more challenges, some seemingly insurmountable, would follow. And their resolutions wouldn't come as easily—or lend themselves to such quaint retellings.

By the end of 1971, however, work was in full bloom, and a business was born. So, too, was my second son, Josh. I couldn't have been happier. But as is often the case when something important is gained, something equally important is lost. That would indeed prove true.

QUILT SHOW

Old, beautifully made quilts were mere sentimental charms until I moved to New York. It was only after my roommate Gayle Gunderman and I began mixing with people in the art world that I discovered how valuable and rare the textiles truly were. So, too, was our unique knowledge of them, gained merely by having grown up around them. Thus, a collaboration of buying/selling/trading quilts was born. And it was that textile-focused business—and the decorative patchwork boudoir pillows that grew from it—that paved the way for Peacock Alley. I know my attention to textiles' overall artistry stems from those early days. Here's what I've learned along the way.

BUYING/COLLECTING: Those of us who love old quilts are usually in one of two groups: the don't-touch-don't-wash collectors and the let's-use-them bunch (which I fall into). And while I certainly admire museum-quality textiles, I favor owning ones that aren't as old or rare but instead mean something to me because of their unique design or history. Even new ones appeal to me. Coveted ones range from "samplers" (think quilted as if it were a box of chocolates, with a uniquely made design in each square), to appliquéd quilts (accented with, say, overscaled tulips or wreaths), to ones featuring kaleidoscopic stars bursting with postage stamp-size fabric pieces, to "crazy" quilts with randomly placed scraps. Depending on pattern, age and quality, color and stitching (the finest quilts being about 20 stitches per inch), they'll cost from a couple hundred dollars to a few thousand.

DISPLAYING: Quilts are made to be used, so I believe the most respectful place to display one is on a bed. A neutral matelassé or lace spread easily complements a colorful quilt, but since most old quilts are too small for today's larger beds, the vintage textiles look best folded in thirds at the foot

of the bed. You can hang them on bracketed rods with curtain ring clips or present a quilt in an acrylic shadowbox. Quilts also make fun tablecloths. I keep red and white ones for just that purpose.

CLEANING: If you plan to sell an old quilt, collectors advise not to wash them. But if you like using quilts, it's OK to gently wash them occasionally. Add about one-half cup of Ivory Snow, Dreft or anything geared to babies to a tub of cold water. Let the cleanser thoroughly dissolve before adding the quilt. Carefully knead the quilt in the soapy water and after about 10 minutes drain the tub of water. Delicately knead out as much water from the quilt as possible but do not wring. Place the quilt on a bed of thick towels and top it with another layer of thick towels; press to absorb water. Then, take it outside and hang it over a clean and taut heavy-gauge-steel line (the quilt will be too heavy for clothespins). Note: If the line is rusty, place the quilt atop an old sheet. Or dry the quilt using the gentlest cycle. Quilts can also be dry cleaned.

STORING: Keep them in clean, cool, dry and dark areas to prevent fading. Extreme temperature changes can cause the fabric to become brittle; 65-70 degrees with 40- to 50-percent humidity is ideal. To prevent yellowed creases, eliminate sharp folds by rolling the quilt in a clean cotton or muslin sheet or in acid-free tissue paper, and store inside an acid-free box. Linen chests or deep drawers also work well. Just don't use airtight plastic bags or cardboard boxes; linens need air circulation. Air your quilt periodically for a day or so before returning it to storage, folded in a slightly different way to keep it pliable and beautiful.

4 COMMITMENT

Once you make a decision, the universe conspires to make it happen.

—RALPH WALDO EMERSON

Before long, every closet and drawer at home was overflowing with boudoir pillows, and Gayle was practically swimming in fabric samples. We were in deep but there was barely time for us to even stop and think about what we had created. The orders kept coming.

By the end of 1971, we decided a toast to our accomplishments was in order during one of my visits to New York City. We opted for an elegant lunch at what was then one of *the* places to see and be seen: Peacock Alley, at the Waldorf-Astoria Hotel. After a few glasses of wine we were especially happy—so much so that the name of our as-yet-unincorporated business was right in front of us: Peacock Alley. How classic, we thought. It signified beauty but wouldn't lock us into any one type of product. Peacock Alley. It was perfect. And so we agreed. It would be our brand—whatever it might grow into.

Michael, who had numerous contacts in the luxury-goods market, introduced me to Sybil Wilkins in early 1972. The former linen buyer for

Peacock Alley

PROMENADE
APRIL • 1943

WHAT'S GOING ON
Theatre
Movies
Music
Art
Sports

...ertainment
...ervice Men

...G ISSUE
...elaer Thayer
...czernin
...Pellman
...ray

Neiman Marcus had recently retired to open a beautifully curated show-room in the Dallas Trade Mart. Sybil had made a name for herself directing Neiman's supremely elegant linen department, so she knew almost everyone who was anyone in the home-textiles business. She also knew our pillows had been in demand since the retailer's Fête des Fleurs Fortnight one year earlier.

For us to truly succeed, we would have to expand our buyer base. That was something Sybil said she could help with as our first sales rep—if we in turn continued making a well-crafted pillow with varied patterns that remained true to its original design. That was agreed on, and I for one was delighted, not only because of Sybil's influence in the home-design industry, but also because we had hit it off instantly, as if longtime friends. Sybil's positive impact on Peacock Alley was almost immediate. We couldn't get those pillows made fast enough.

Business became steady and brisk enough for us to lease our first production space in an industrial area of North Dallas. It was no-frills, but it was ours. Designer Audrey Friedman, who would go on to be a major name in the world of table linens, shared the warehouse with us, along with our first commercial sewing machine and first full-time employee, seamstress Sylvia Guerrero. Meanwhile, recognition for our pillows was increasing, as were orders. For the first time in our 10-year collaboration, Gayle and I began seeing money come in—not enough to retire on, but just enough to have something to put back into the business.

By this time, Michael and I had grown even closer with Gayle and Marty, whose children were nearly the same ages as Jason and Josh. We often visited them at their home in East Hampton and farm in New Jersey. It seemed fitting that toward the end of a very long and productive year, Gayle and I finally cemented our working relationship on October 1,

1973, by officially incorporating Peacock Alley.

With the company based in Dallas, I would need to continue carrying most of the workload—managing production and a growing staff as well as selling and promoting. Gayle would continue selling and sourcing fabrics. To account for each share of the work, we decided I would hold 75 percent interest in the business, and Gayle 25 percent. We also commissioned design of a logo, one that did not refer in an obvious way to a peacock so as to not seem predictable. We chose instead to include in the logo a lilac, which will always remind me of my mother and the many years I cut lilacs for her on Mother's Day and May Day. I'm glad we did that; she was touched by the sentiment.

As for my own motherhood, I was doing my best to mind two very young, very active sons. My business life was frenzied, but it did afford me freedom to keep up with them more often than not. So I had no thoughts of returning to the brokerage business, which I viewed as a past adventure. I had moved on to a new challenge, one testing my creativity and stamina in a market that I could see was just beginning to boom. (In 1974, a record-breaking $800 million in sheets and pillowcases were sold in the U.S.)

Accomplishing the seemingly never-ending tasks needed to make our new business profitable and respected only increased my appetite for success. During that time, I was rather harried, reviewing incoming invoices, creating outgoing paperwork and examining every inch of our pillows alongside Sylvia, who by then was helping guide the work of several other seamstresses. She and I insisted that fabric selection and stitching be exceptional, and we often worked late into the night. My energy and drive seemed to come out of nowhere, and it fed a strong sense of self-worth. I was my own boss, and succeeding. That was the feeling the men in my family had relished. Now it was my turn.

LEFT) From New York to Dallas, it became clear early on that Peacock Alley would embody the kind of simple yet elegant luxury I'd admired for years—and still do. One of my favorite indulgences is a platter of oysters on the half shell and a crisp white wine shared with friends at our home on Martha's Vineyard.

By early 1974 Sybil deemed Peacock Alley pillows ready for their first showing at the New York Gift Fair. And she had even bigger plans to discuss with us. The relationship we had forged with Neiman's—our biggest buyer and greatest champion—was priceless, she said, for us and also for any home-fashions manufacturing powerhouse that might want to join forces with us. If we could figure out a way to partner with one of the major domestic mills respected by Neiman Marcus, we could be well on our way to national, even international, sales and acclaim. For this to be, however, we'd need to think beyond making boudoir pillows. We'd need to think bedding, period.

That would be a huge leap for our little pillow company, requiring a new way of designing products and doing business—and, of course, a major influx of revenue. But Sybil was convinced this was possible. If Gayle and I were intimidated by such a prospect, it wouldn't be for long. Sybil's confidence, along with her outstanding reputation in the home-textiles world, inspired us to take a deep breath and dive in. After helping devise a business concept we could actually deliver on, Sybil arranged not only for our entrée into the New York Gift Fair, but also for an appointment with the president of Wamsutta Mills, a fortuitous meeting that would help set Peacock Alley in a fashionable new direction.

Prior to the mid-1970s, bedding had served a utilitarian purpose, much as early quilts had. In the grandest houses, a bedroom's distinction was marked by an antique bed or a tufted headboard, sometimes accompanied by a monogrammed blanket cover, or a floral bedspread designed to coordinate with drapery. Otherwise, bedding options were limited in design and supply at regional specialty stores (which themselves were limited). Accordingly, major domestic mills such as Wamsutta, Martex, Fieldcrest and J.P. Stevens were selling only sheets and pillow cases, nothing more.

Peacock Alley aimed to change all of that, and did.

The void was obvious to me. We spend nearly a third of our lives sleeping, yet not one company in this country was concentrating on making fashion-forward items for the bed, such as coverlets, pillow shams and bedskirts—accessories commonly found in Europe's nicer homes and luxury hotels and inns. Few, if any, American companies were providing stylish bedding ensembles for stylishly dressed women. It made sense to me that these women would want to dress their bedrooms as they dressed themselves: in natural fibers, simple silhouettes and classic colors. It was how I dressed, and it was how I wanted to live.

The most innovative introduction in bedding had been Wamsutta's creation in the late 1960s of "supercale," a beautifully finished poly-cotton sheeting that stayed relatively wrinkle-free. By the early 1970s many women, inspired by home décor magazines, had begun using sheeting for wall coverings and upholstery. Sold in wide swaths, the sheeting provided seamless looks. As a plus, it was more affordable than other broadloom fabrics available in, say, heavy silk or linen. Such "achievable luxury" applications had caught the attention of the major mills, but they weren't quite sure how to proceed. We were.

During our meeting with Wamsutta, Sybil, Gayle and I managed to convince them they needed a fashion twist for their sheeting. (As far as anyone knows, Peacock Alley was the first small, boudoir-focused company to do so with a major mill.) In our plan, Peacock Alley would buy sheeting fabric of Wamsutta's fashion prints and get an exclusive on using it to design coordinating accessories such as bed skirts, blanket covers, shams and decorative pillows, hanger covers and bedside caddies. It all would be sold through Neiman Marcus, who in turn would make a splash with our products in its popular *Pink Sale* linen catalog.

Former broker puts stock in patchwork

By DOROTHY FAGG
Staff Writer

Patchwork pillows worked a change in Mary Ella Needleman's life.

Four years ago she was an accredited stockbroker, employed in Dallas. Today she is designer and president of Peacock Alley, a high fashion bedroom linens company. She guides the industry here in Dallas, seeing it grow to sales of more than $700,000 this year. Her New York partner, Gayle Gordon, joins her in creating unusual designs for the upper-line company. Their designs, she says, are planned to complement ready-to-wear fashion trends as well as those in linens.

The two began with only patchwork.

"WE STARTED the business with one customer, Robert Goodman Antiques," Mrs. Needleman says. "From there we have grown."

Choosing a name for their bedroom ensembles line posed problems for them. "We thought of Pillows Inc. since

pillows were our first item to sell. But that seemed to limit us too much. We feel that the name Peacock Alley places no limitation on our expanding to other linens."

Peacock Alley has gained exclusive rights to Dior Rose pattern by Wamsutta fabrics.

"MY HUSBAND, Michael, who is a manufacturers' representative, has helped us with lots of our ideas and has helped us solve many of our problems." Mrs. Needleman says. "He is from Boston and we met in New York."

Mary Ella Needleman looks astonished when queried about hobbies. "Our work," she replies. "And we try to spend lots of time with our two little boys, Josh and Jason. No, I don't sew for them. They wear jeans, thank goodness."

Caption: PRESIDENT and designer of Peacock Alley, Mrs. Michael Needleman contemplates one of the embroidered lacey pillows which has catapulted the two-year-old company into a booming business.

Home tour to aid Bradfield school

The tour of Highland Park homes will be a fund-raising project for Bradfield School. Tickets may be purchased for the Friday tour from Mrs. Sam P. Burford Jr., 4515 Arcady. Hours of the tour are 10 a.m. to 2 p.m.

Dr. and Mrs. Ray Lawson's house at 4201 Versailles, first on the tour, is an authentic Spanish home built 45 years ago by architect George Dahl. The Lawsons have added many antiques and treasures.

The Bill Cooper home, 4425 Versailles, looks like true Williamsburg. Goodwin-Tatum, architects, went to Williamsburg to study design before building the house and Jerry Oden has designed the interior.

The house of Dr. and Mrs. J. T. Hatfield at 4225 Fairfax is

an authentic English Tudor house, which is furnished with many antiques and paintings.

The Hammond Hopkins house at 6019 St. Andrews looks as if it might be found on a French Normandy lane. Antique accessories have been collected by Mr. and Mrs. Hopkins through the years and Joe Chastain helped design the interior. Crewel pieces were done by Mrs. Hopkins' aunt. Berns and Shelmire did the extensive remodeling at the rear of the house.

Mr. and Mrs. Mack Pogue's home at 4293 Bordeaux blends English Tudor with today's bright contemporary colors chosen by Jerry Oden. Behind the living room is a family room and the cabana almost fills the back yard.

LEFT) A story that appeared in 1971 in *The Dallas Morning News* when I first launched Peacock Alley.
BELOW) A Polaroid of the original patchwork and lace pillows ready to be shipped for Neiman Marcus' Fête des Fleurs event.

Though Wamsutta's leaders eagerly embraced the idea of producing accessories, execution of this plan would be difficult. Most of the mill's salesmen were accustomed to selling only sheets. They didn't have a clue about using them to dress an entire bedroom. Clearly they thought that was the responsibility of a woman—but that it was not a woman's place to make business decisions alongside them. I was in an industry dominated by men and change would come slowly.

By 1975 I was working nonstop, and Peacock Alley was getting a lot of attention. Everything appeared to be falling into place. Everything except my marriage, which was coming apart at the seams.

My fast-growing career was more than Michael had bargained for: He'd wanted a loving wife and children and a beautiful home—and had attained them. But included in that package was a strong wife, one who worked. That wouldn't have been a problem had I simply adjusted my life to make his traveling and entertaining interests my priority. But the more success I tasted, the less I wanted to give up work and do that. Sadly, the stronger I became, the more distance grew between us. What little time I did have was directed toward our sons' happiness, then Michael's, then mine. I had hoped things would get better between us once Peacock Alley was on solid footing. But by 1976, our marriage had ended in divorce.

Our decision to go separate ways was a big disappointment, but not a surprise. A year earlier, I'd begun to think I might become the boys' primary means of support, so I had quietly braced myself for that. I also became more determined than ever to make Peacock Alley work. Divorce wasn't something I'd seriously considered until then; it wasn't really in my family's vocabulary. But Michael and I each wanted out. And for the sake of Jason, then 6, and Josh, 4, I didn't want the split to be contentious

PEACOCK ALLEY: A 'SWELL' HISTORY

The Waldorf-Astoria's lavish lobby restaurant, favored by A-list celebrities and power brokers since its opening in 1964, had gotten its name, Peacock Alley, from a 300-foot-long alley that once joined two Astor family hotels—the Waldorf and the Astoria (Fifth Avenue between 33rd and 34th Streets).

After both opulent hotels opened in the late 1890s, the *New York Herald*'s society editor delighted in watching the "swells," or the beautiful people, traversing the promenade in the very finest of fashions. Legend has it maître d' Oscar Tschirky (creator of the famous Waldorf salad) remarked, "Look at them, strutting and preening along that corridor. Just like peacocks"—to which the editor replied, "Not a bad name … Peacock Alley. Mind if I call it that in the paper tomorrow?" The name stuck.

A family dispute over which hotel would out-best the other led to the razing of both hotels in 1929 to make way for the Empire State Building. With money received for the property, the family opened one hotel grander than all others—the Waldorf-Astoria, at Lexington Avenue at 49th and 50th Streets.

The art deco hotel's splendid foyer, which took the name Peacock Alley, attracted tens of thousands of visitors a day, including when an American president was in residence. Though the style and grandeur of the esteemed restaurant has changed over the years, its mission to impress with luxury prevails. As does ours.

and wanted to preserve a sense of family. They adored their father, and he adored them; I didn't want anything to change that.

Major physical and emotional hurdles arose, however, when Michael, then only 36, was hit by a series of strokes. Recovery would be slow, we learned, and he would need physical therapy, preferably with his children at his side. The angst over this development was almost unbearable; Michael and I had already decided to part, and we did.

Our breakup undoubtedly came as a shock to the boys, since we had never argued in front of them. Somehow, though, they accepted it. In the years following our divorce, Michael and I gained a new appreciation for each another. Our children provided a strong connection between us and we communicated regularly about it. We both wanted them to feel our caring and love for them even though we were no longer married.

I did learn some hard lessons, the most important being to never use your husband's attorney to negotiate your divorce. I was offered no

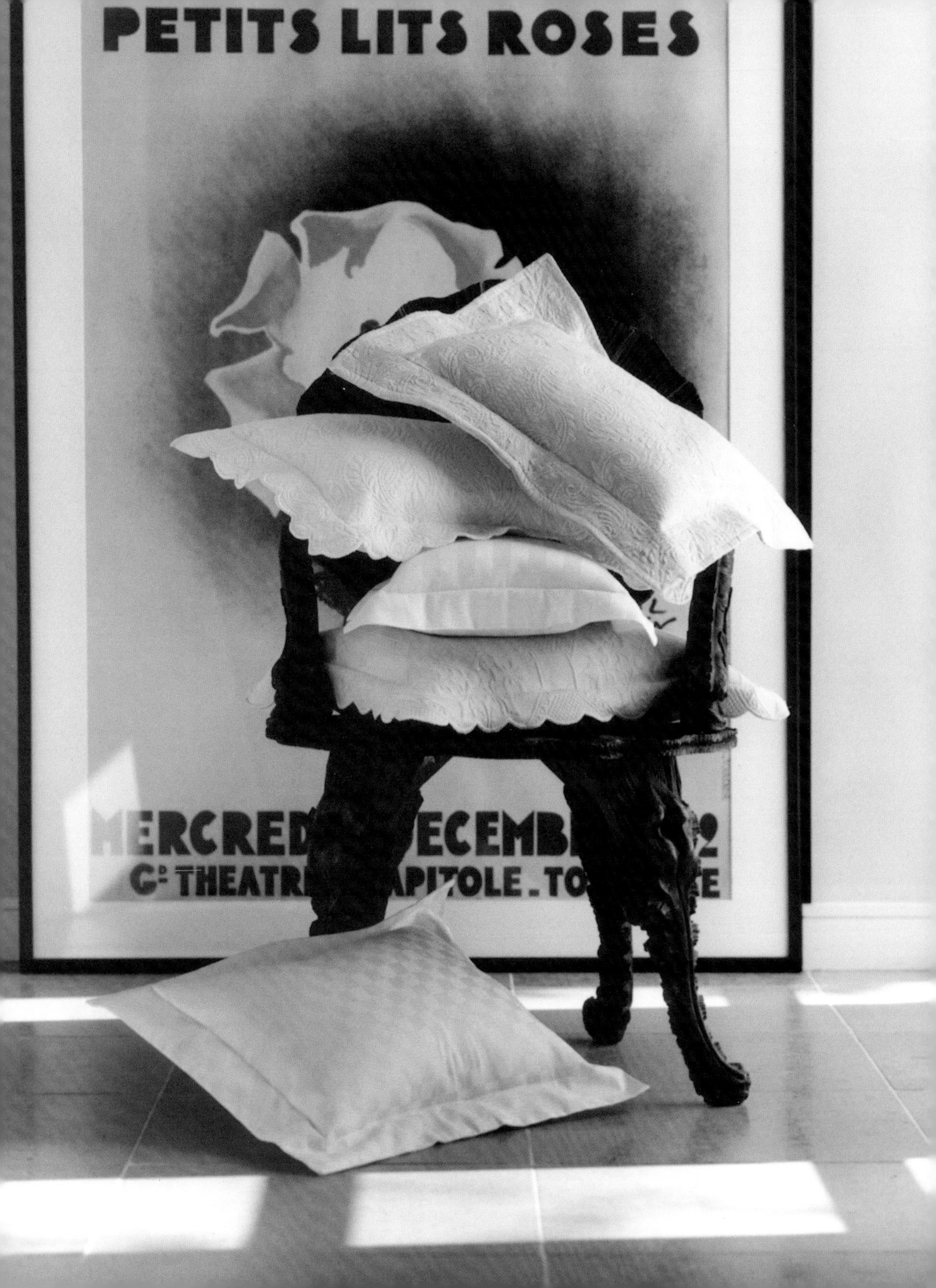
PETITS LITS ROSES

alimony and only a small amount per month per child, just enough to cover my housing costs. For us to survive I'd need to start taking money out of my young business. That meant I'd have to work harder than ever, which seemed almost impossible in light of my already considerable workload.

To show support, my parents came to Dallas. They stayed with us for awhile to help me figure out my next steps. I was grateful for that, and for them. One positive to come from that ordeal was that we all grew closer. They'd always given me, as their daughter, a sense of security, but as a mother I felt that even more so—not because they gave me money or things, but because they let me know they'd always be there for me. I've tried to do that for my own children ever since.

At 35, I became a single mother struggling to keep two sons thriving and a business surviving. I moved myself and the boys into a much smaller home in Dallas' University Park, an established, family-oriented neighborhood with a good public school system. Next I would need to rearrange

LEFT) A photo of me, around the time I met Ray, in the mid-1970s. **BELOW)** President Gerald Ford and Ray Gabler aboard Air Force One, during the time Ray was running for Congress.

my life to allow for both work and family time. I was particularly blessed when our nannie, Ymelda Perez, agreed to stay on with us since she didn't want to lose ties with Jason and Josh. Moreover, several good friends with sons in the same after-school activities as the boys often helped with transportation needs. I smile when I think about how at several events when asked where I was, Jason and Josh would say I was working in a factory. In a way, of course, that was true. But I had to keep going. Failure wasn't part of the equation.

Creating bedding accessories from concept to consumer raves was richly gratifying and exhilarating. The first products Peacock Alley produced for Wamsutta were in keeping with the day's fashion, which might be described best as Americana chic: white eyelet shams and bedskirts, with blanket covers in accenting gingham, sophisticated botanicals and blue and white porcelain. (The first floral pattern to spring to mind is Wamsutta's Dior Rose, among the best-selling sheet patterns of all time.)

Our success with Wamsutta did not go unnoticed by our competition, which soon was nipping at our heels and also knocking on the doors of Wamsutta and others to forge similar relationships. Gayle and I realized all of our proverbial eggs were in one basket, which is never good. We needed to develop our products and create more of an identity for Peacock Alley, and if we wanted to stay at least two steps ahead of our competitors—which we knew might one day be Wamsutta itself—we'd have to diversify. So we began to design our own bedding line for specialty stores, bedding a cut above what we had been making with sheeting materials. Our signature eyelet lace was integral to the first products we'd made, but we became highly selective of any printed cotton fabrics we used. Nothing branded Peacock Alley should look run-of-the-mill or mass-

LEFT) This is a piece of antique English Battenberg lace, a style that inspired our early bedding. The handmade lace collections we produced helped solidify our position as a luxury linens maker.

market, which had become the industry norm. Peacock Alley would need to become associated more with luxury, but accessibly so.

To further differentiate us, we introduced sumptuous bedding ensembles made of intricate Nottingham lace. But the age-old, super-fine English lace hadn't been imported but rather made in New England on actual Nottingham lace looms. The dusty machines had once anchored a lace factory that had gone under at the start of the easy-care, low-cost bedding craze. I convinced a distributor we worked with to bring the factory back to life by cleaning and calibrating the looms, and reemploying the England-trained technicians who'd moved to the U.S. specifically to operate the machines. Investing in the lace's return—in blanket covers and shams made from two different patterns—was rewarded when Ethan Allen ordered our distinctive line for many of its stores throughout the country.

More change in direction for Peacock Alley came with help from Raymond Gabler, whom I'd gotten to know and trust over several years when he was Wamsutta's Southwest territory sales manager. Ray recently had gone solo, opening his own wholesale showroom selling soft goods—home-furnishings products—in Dallas' World Trade Center. Ray decided to become a consultant, which couldn't have come at a better time for Peacock Alley. We had lost our friend and mentor Sybil to a devastating illness. Our sales and marketing compass had been lost. Ray offered to step in to help however he could.

Ray was tall, handsome, charismatic, outgoing and larger than life—the consummate politician. In fact, he narrowly missed being just that, losing a congressional race during the late 1960s in the Texas Hill Country home district of President Lyndon B. Johnson. The fact that Ray, a Republican, won 47 percent of the vote in his bid was impressive, especially in a solidly

Democratic region. The next-best career for him was in marketing and sales, in which his winning personality helped him excel.

I didn't think much about Ray at first. But after his marriage began faltering, and mine had dissolved, we leaned on each other for support. We began seeing each other, which I enjoyed immensely (Jason and Josh, too; Ray, himself a father, was outdoorsy and fun). As a sales leader he'd been a big champion of my work, but now, as a close friend, he wanted only to focus on our happiness. Ray was destined to be a great love—and a great support during the most brutal chapter of my life and career.

THREAD OF CONTINUITY

Too often in business we don't seek help until we're on the verge of throwing in the towel. I desperately didn't want to do that. I did want to find a seamstress who wasn't just talented, exceptionally so, but one who could share my vision and work ethic during my business' critical make-or-break period. Who I found, through a newspaper classified ad, was Sylvia Guerrero.

Sylvia's easygoing and fun style, creative mind and deft skill served as the perfect antidote for any worries I had about succeeding. "No problem," she said at the time, surveying my pleading eyes and disaster-zone sewing room. "We'll make it."

Perhaps because of our immediate connection, I believed her. Within a day she was working alongside me in my home sewing room. And after that November 1970 afternoon, she would continue giving me reason to believe we'd make it—for 42 years. Peacock Alley's first and longest-serving employee retired in 2012. Through good times and bad, we've remained close friends and always will.

When we met, Sylvia was the mother of a son Jason's age and a daughter Josh's age. We found a lot to talk about while dedicating ourselves to creating beautiful pillows as our children played together within sight.

"I'd always enjoyed sewing, mostly clothing and tabletop décor, and I was good at it. Many believed very good at it," Sylvia told me shortly after she retired. "But I'd never seen anything as decorative and precise as what you were doing." She was right. Our patchwork pillows would be a challenge for even the most experienced sewers. Gayle and I, novice sewers, had needed a year to get them right. "They were so meticulously made," Sylvia recalled. She had always admired quilts but had never made one and was unfamiliar with their multi-layered construction. She said, "I had to learn fast, but to be careful, very careful. It wasn't like we were just sewing for ourselves. A lot of nice stores were buying what we were making. And we were always watching the clock. It was very important that orders be filled well and on time."

I was greatly impressed with Sylvia's sewing knowledge, which she'd acquired from her mother while growing up in Monterrey, Mexico. She'd strengthened those skills in her early days as an immigrant trying to make it in America, crafting almost everything she and her children wanted to wear but couldn't afford. The self-assuredness Sylvia gained from those accomplishments only helped boost my own confidence as we moved ahead.

In 1973, Peacock Alley moved into its first production space. With increased sales, we began hiring more help, which meant Sylvia would be lead trainer. And as I'd learned while trying to find someone of Sylvia's talent, it wasn't easy locating someone who could quickly catch on, have the necessary exactness and sense of urgency—and stay on.

Sylvia's sense of humor got us through tedious tasks; I remember us laughing as we made a blanket cover we had designed for Sakowitz, one with exaggerated buttonholes that had to be hand-threaded with ribbons that didn't want to stay in position. Or when Neiman Marcus owner Stanley Marcus came back from a trip with some wrapping-paper-like, silkscreened fabric and asked us to make pillows with it.

My partnership with Sylvia worked like this: I'd have an idea for a new design but wouldn't know exactly how to implement it. Sylvia would give it a shot, and I'd start to finesse it—or try to. If my ideas weren't working, I welcomed her ideas. Peacock Alley makes the best-made domestic products in the industry today, and I'm firm in attributing that to Sylvia's expertise, dedication and friendship.

FASHION FORWARD

Our continuing commitment to building strong business relationships was greatly influenced by Bill Williams, one of Neiman Marcus' most gifted minds. Bill was their linen buyer when we first met; he'd later direct its hugely successful mail-order business, and later became CEO of Harry & David. His skillful way of listening and questioning, his trust in our abilities, and his belief in our creative goals would in turn inspire us. Thank you, Bill. And thanks, too, for sharing your thoughts on those early days together:

Peacock Alley's style reflected a bespoke fashion sensibility in bedding that up to that point was non-existent. When I first met Mary Ella in 1974, it was apparent she had a definite point of view about aesthetics. At that time many women were into flamboyant fashions and big hair, but Mary Ella exuded understated elegance. I picture her in a beautifully tailored gray wool suit with high lace-collar blouse, her hair simple and chic. In essence, her style matched exactly the product she was selling—classic good taste.

Peacock Alley also was riding the crest of the new wave of dressing a bedroom in a personalized way, with pillow shams, dust ruffles and blanket covers, while offering everything you could ever possibly want for comfort— bedside caddies, for instance, even elbow pillows. Also brilliant was how their products could really fit into anyone's bedroom, be it understated Colonial or high-boudoir. Peacock Alley led the way in helping people understand they didn't need to completely redo a bedroom to give it a fresh, new look in a way that was luxurious yet affordable.

We took a risk on Peacock Alley because we saw they were doing something revolutionary. We also could see they had impeccable character personally. They never failed us.

5 STRENGTH

Once we truly know that life is difficult—
once we truly understand and accept it—
then life is no longer difficult.

—M. SCOTT PECK

S weet-talking Texan Ray Gabler, fun and unpredictable, quite literally swept me off my feet. On weekend country-and-western
music jaunts, he was determined to teach me the cotton-eyed Joe
and Texas two-step—and I was a willing student.

Ray's ability to sway almost anyone into the lap of luxury was legendary.
His inimitable, down-to-earth sophistication in the sales and marketing
of soft-home goods contributed to the success that allowed him to leave
Wamsutta in the mid-1970s to open Raymond F. Gabler and Associates.
In this "one-stop shop for a better shop" in the Dallas World Trade Center,
he represented such clients as Palais Royal, Spirella, Down Inc. and, of
course, Peacock Alley.

Benefiting from Ray's impeccable connections and creative thinking,
Peacock Alley was becoming more widely known for our unique balance
of feminine and modern, soft and sweet—but not overwrought—romantic.

OPPOSITE) The Victorian house that Ray and I bought together and restored, and where we had our wedding reception. We didn't know it was haunted by a previous owner, Mr. Bryan, until we'd signed the papers and been given the keys! Strange things happened, like throw rugs being moved around in the middle of the night and the kitchen door opening and slamming by itself, but nothing too scary.

Twelve years my senior, Ray was a source of wisdom, companionship and comfort. Our bond was a blessed thing, especially after the unraveling of our marriages and the resulting emotional tolls. We shared so many of the same interests, even a fondness for heirloom linens. Ray was tough but also tender, and he was the first man to ever nurture my creative side, which fueled it even more.

With Lone Star roots that ran deep, Ray enjoyed playing gentleman squire. Our long Sunday afternoon drives culminated in coppery sunsets and enriched spirits. On one weekend outing, we drove to Granbury, about 40 miles southwest of Fort Worth. Just off the old town square we saw for sale a two-story Victorian house that was the very picture of old Texas. As we toured the 11-room place inside and out, we exchanged looks that confirmed our hunch: This was it. This was the house we could see ourselves sharing.

To test our instincts we made an offer, though a ridiculously low one, just

for the fun of it. That offer, of course, was rejected. We were initially disappointed but we made a pact to stick to it. And then, several months later, the homeowners called to inquire if we were still interested. Indeed, we were.

At the closing, we learned the home had a previously undisclosed occupant, the ghost of, apparently, Mr. Bryan, the home's builder and original owner. I was scared to death. Ray wasn't. But things did get interesting after we witnessed some peculiar incidents.

Fortunately Mr. Bryan was a friendly ghost who apparently liked hanging around in the stairwell. And moving things around. And playing with light switches, alarm clocks and area rugs.

I vividly recall feeling his presence one afternoon. While dusting the staircase balustrade, I felt as if I was being watched. Then, a cold chill. I decided to take a stand. "If you're going to show yourself, Mr. Bryan, do it now," I said nicely but firmly. "Please don't scare me and make me have a heart attack."

After that, all was calm, enough so that on July 12, 1980, when Ray and I married in Granbury's little Episcopal church, we weren't worried about hosting the wedding reception in our home. Presumably, Mr. Bryan was in attendance.

Ray had already raised a family, with older children now married themselves. I wasn't sure if he really wanted to go through the parenting process again with Jason and Josh, then 11 and 9. But Ray was a natural father who treated my sons as if they were his own. He was definitely stricter than Michael. Michael's world offered go-karts and expensive toys, many from the high-end companies he represented. Ray was all about the outdoors and getting his hands dirty. The influence of both men, however, provided good balance for the boys, who would learn to appreciate both ways of living.

Ray carried a secret ambition. He had grown up in south Texas on a

ABOVE) Ray and I bought some land in Acton after we were married, which came with a run-down old farmhouse free of charge, which we fixed up. We added a porch that wrapped around three sides, and because we were on a hill, there was a nice breeze blowing—we'd sit in our antique wicker furniture and have mint juleps.

LEFT) The original farm house as it looked in 1980.

cotton farm later wiped out by a hurricane. Ever since, he had yearned to be a farmer—in his case, a gentleman farmer—to live simply off the land, reconnecting with who he really was, or at least wanted to be. In 1982 he found just the place to realize his dream. The property, in the Acton countryside about 10 miles northeast of Granbury, comprised 54 acres of rolling terrain with old thickets of shade trees and a winding creek. And though the land was indeed beautiful, I was not pleased with Ray's new-found love. For one thing, we were just beginning to enjoy our Granbury home, now completely outfitted, and we'd need to sell in order to buy the land and its 120-year-old ramshackle farmhouse. But Ray insisted this "once-in-a-lifetime opportunity" was perfect for us. And what could I say? He had a charming way of selling beautiful things.

On weekends we'd take the boys to help us clear fallen brush and trees, repair fences, paint, rewire, replumb and generally make the house structurally sound by rebuilding it from the inside out. It was work I wouldn't wish on anyone. Ray, on the other hand, loved it.

I'd known the farming life to some extent in those early years spent visiting my mother's parents' farms, which were much more idyllic than our recently acquired hardscrabble one. This realization was even more painfully obvious thanks to the niceties we'd grown accustomed to in our lines of work. So for me, our new endeavor was truly a "Green Acres" experience.

My first meltdown occurred in the kitchen while washing my hair under the rusty old sink's faucet, the only one in the house that worked. With my head bent down, I noticed something out of the corner of my eye. It was moving across the floor. Actually, slithering across the floor. I panicked and shrieked, "Snake!" In a flash, Ray was at the rescue. With a shotgun. The bull snake didn't have a chance, but neither did our kitchen wall, which suddenly had a large hole with a view to the outside. "Just another way to commune with nature," Ray said with a wink.

After most of the necessary repairs to the house were complete, one of the last things we did was renovate and expand the home's porch, making it wraparound-style to increase our outdoor living space. We dined out there and even slept out there (though I always kept a watchful eye for low-lying visitors). It was difficult to envision at the time, but restoring what we called simply "The Farm" to a place of peace would, during the difficult days ahead, help restore our own sense of peace.

On work days in Dallas, Peacock Alley's day-to-day operations were stable enough for me to embark on a five-year business venture with my good friend Joan Kramer. Joan and I connected on several levels: Both of us moved in the same home-furnishings circles (she was a trade publication editor) and we'd both grown up in the Appalachian Valley area, began our careers in New York and moved with our husbands to Dallas to start our families.

These commonalities, including a shared sense of style, inspired us to open a small shop full of the things we ourselves loved to buy. Gabler & Kramer sold antique and vintage-style home décor as well as natural-fiber clothing and accessories. Dallas-Fort Worth Home & Garden described our Highland Park Village boutique as "a nostalgic wonderland of lovely sleepwear, satin slippers, antique silver and soft-sculpture accessories. Sheets and coverlets are gently shaded in soft pastels and dusty tones, printed in traditional floral patterns and trimmed with yards of delicate lace."

Gabler & Kramer would be a great practice-run for Peacock Alley's namesake boutiques in the decade ahead. And, quite simply, the sideline

ABOVE) During the 1980s, Joan Kramer and I owned a linen and lingerie store in Highland Park Village in Dallas called Gabler & Kramer. This portrait of us ran in the High Profile section of *The Dallas Morning News*, which meant we'd really made it; we were open about eight years. **RIGHT)** As fashions evolved, we replaced lace with intricate embroidery in styles such as Opera, this lovely sheeting line crafted in Italy.

venture was fun; it also was a terrific way to more directly connect with Peacock Alley's client base. Decidedly, though, my true focus was on developing Peacock Alley's own style. In the spring and summer of 1982 that style included blue-and-white seersucker bedding for a traditional nod, but also balanced with more-modern-minded sheets featuring a subtle beige-and-white print.

By then we'd formed our trademark look—natural fabrics with pale or muted colors accented with crisp white and plenty of lace. Such design supported my observation in the *Dallas Times Herald* that people were tiring of the huge quilted floral bedspreads that had been so hot—in popularity but also in non-breathable, heavyweight material.

We sought to keep the bedroom beautiful, but simply so. "Consumers want a choice of items for the home that can provide the flexibility to mix with a variety of hand-me-down antiques and more streamlined contemporary furniture," I told the *Times Herald*. The article also highlighted my take on the bedroom's changing role as a more private and soothing retreat, a second living space.

I smile now thinking how these design ideas were being discussed three decades ago. It very well could have been yesterday. We were committed—and remain committed—to better living through better bedding. That's what would set us apart from the major mills, and still does.

By the end of 1982, Peacock Alley's unique aesthetic approach appeared to be working, with each season's new and classic bedding lines carried by 500 specialty and department stores, from Neiman Marcus and its mail-order Horchow Collection, to Saks Fifth Avenue, Marshall Field's, Sakowitz and I. Magnin. But why wouldn't business be going well? Wasn't it true that the harder you worked, the stronger your business became? I thought so. The year 1983, however, would be a game-changer.

PAGE 134) In early 2000, we crafted our signature Vienna matelassé in silk, shown here in lush Chocolate.

LEFT) The same rich Vienna Silk was downright seductive in white.

Five years after China had opened its borders to foreign companies and began pursuing more trade, much had started to happen. U.S. companies were beginning to take their manufacturing overseas, where wages were 85 percent less than in the U.S. and tax incentives were bountiful.

The U.S. economy was in recession, but the home-goods market had remained stable enough for us not to worry, or too much, at least. That's often the case during down economic times, when people invest less in outside interests and more in decorating their homes. Ray and I had been hearing about Chinese lace from wholesale buyers but dismissed it; Chinese exports had a specific audience, and it wasn't ours.

Or so I thought. One afternoon during a visit to a World Trade Center showroom in Dallas, I knew we were in trouble. The Battenberg-style lace I held in my hand was a cheaply made knockoff; anyone with any knowledge of old lace could see that. But I also knew that most people wouldn't

realize it. Or they'd at least overlook it, especially since the lace was hand-made, and at a fraction of the cost of European lace. U.S. retailers would be clamoring to save money while not appearing to cut quality.

We were in trouble. Our fine Nottingham-style lace, made in New England, as well as laces we imported from Europe, were such an essential part of the Peacock Alley look they made up almost half of our business.

Before our ship could take on too much water, Gayle and I took strategic action. After learning that Ethan Allen had dropped us in favor of creating its own bedding with the Chinese lace, our first line of defense was clear: We'd need to start de-emphasizing lace. But what a heartbreaking realization; we had invested into it so much financial and emotional capital. Within a year, our worst fears would come true. We'd suffer a 50-percent drop in revenue.

Our next course of action became clear during that year's Paris Textile Show, as we wandered the aisles looking for any design idea or textile that could give us a competitive edge. European style was, and is, an enduring and classic inspiration, so there had been plenty of beauty but no revelations. That is, until almost by divine intervention we met the owners of a small Italian textile mill with a name we'd yet to hear—Bruna. Its product was some of the finest cotton sheeting we'd seen in the Italian market. It was nothing short of exquisite compared to percale, which most of the U.S. market was buying. Only Wamsutta was still selling all-cotton sheets, but barely.

We sighed, assuming we weren't the only ones aware of Bruna. But we *were* the first—at least in the U.S., where Bruna was eager to do business. Ray and I quickly worked out a deal for Peacock Alley to be their exclusive U.S. distributor. Things were looking up.

As I explained to the Times-Herald at the end of 1983, "Tough economic times have motivated people to invest in quality or not invest at all." That was our hope, at least, and was what we'd counted on after factoring our receivables with a longtime business friend. The cash flow would help us stay afloat as we altered our design direction. What also helped was having our products continue to experience strong catalog sales.

Peacock Alley bedding ensembles became directed toward a European-style aesthetic. We also started offering table linens, home fragrances and other home accessories. That we survived those years still amazes me. In the midst of the ongoing recession, some banks were failing and the ones that weren't were scrutinizing their accounts like hawks, calling in their loans. When Peacock Alley's loan was called in, I wasn't too concerned— we had been on good terms with the bank, always making our payments on time, and our reputation was solid. I was confident I could talk them into letting us pay the loan over time. They, on the other hand, had a more expeditious liquidation plan. They would simply take the stock in a Pennsylvania bank that I'd pledged against the $70,000 balance of the loan—stock that made up a significant portion of my personal savings. I had inherited the stock from my grandfather, and it had meant the world to him. On his watch it had done exceedingly well, and on mine it would disappear.

I was in a dark place. My father had died within the past few years and my mother was very ill. Now, my grandfather's gift, the financial backbone of my hope for the future, had left me feeling rudderless. Frankly, since I had always paid the bank on time, I'd never even considered the possibility of losing the collateral I'd offered against the loan. But the devastating chain of events—the Chinese lace invasion, the loss of my father, Peacock Alley's loan recall, the pending loss of most of my savings—didn't stop there.

The next blow involved my partner and friend, Gayle. In thinking about Peacock Alley's future, I was certain our design talents, business assets, respected reputation and ever-increasing product demand would be the rock on which we could stand and weather the storm. We'd simply need to pool our resources to obtain a commercial bank loan. But Gayle saw things differently. Our setbacks had been too stressful. She was willing to give up her 25 percent interest in Peacock Alley in order to be removed from the bank's loan guarantee.

It was a tremendous let-down. To see the end of such a powerful bond—with a friend who'd been at my side from near girlhood, who'd shared with me countless personal and professional joys and setbacks—was an experience on a par with divorce. In retrospect, though, I understand her decision.

In time I would reap the benefits of being Peacock Alley's sole shareholder, but at that moment the responsibility I faced was scary. I felt

deserted. Ray wasn't in a position to help Peacock Alley financially, but he did provide tremendous emotional support, as did Jason, Josh, Sylvia and other close friends who vowed to help me carry on.

Could I have ridded myself of everything and everyone at Peacock Alley to salvage what I could of my savings? Yes. But I wasn't going to give in. Peacock Alley was in my blood. Against all odds, I had helped create a brand on the verge of being powerful. And the work I was doing, alongside people I loved and admired, was priceless to me.

Parting ways with my money and my best friend, I would search for strength—and better days.

FEATHERING THE NEST

As a child I loved the comfort of sleeping on feather mattresses. I wouldn't appreciate the joy of down comforters until adulthood, when I began traveling abroad. They were known as "eiderdown" or "continental" quilts until "duvet," the French word for "down," came into favor.

In the mid-1960s, Sir Terence Conran introduced duvets to his ground-breaking, trend-setting London home-décor shop, Habitat. Sir Conran said covering the duvet with a washable sheeting fabric, fastened with ties, buttons or a zipper, made it easier to clean the heavy, unwieldy comforter. Duvet covers also allowed for changeable bedding designs, and they eliminated the need for a top sheet, allowing a bed to be made in just a couple of shakes.

Such simplicity wouldn't catch on in the U.S. until 20 years later. Until then, most U.S. consumers favored boldly patterned, perfectly matched, machine-washable, wrinkle-free polyester bedding sets. I realized that Sir Conran was on to something.

Imported duvets and duvet covers had been available only from the highest-end specialty stores, but by the late 1980s our design thinking focused on their luxe look, natural warmth, simple style changeability and easy care, qualities touted in Peacock Alley marketing campaigns. Ironically, we promoted the old-world bedding as innovative (and to the U.S., it was).

Natural duvet covers in soothing neutral colors and simple patterns could give a bedroom a more sophisticated look, making the space a relaxing oasis. Quite simply, slipcovered bedding was, and is, smart.

I'm always pleased when interior designers and retailers recognize Peacock Alley as one of the first to popularize duvet covers in the U.S. I'm also happy to see that, as bedding trends go, this one won't be leaving us anytime soon.

OPPOSITE) My granddaughters Lucy Ray and Mary Eloise feel the same way I do about down on the bed.

6 GROWTH

If you're going through hell, keep going.

—WINSTON CHURCHILL

Maybe this sounds counterintuitive, but when faced with a crisis, I try not to over-think it. During the rebuilding of Peacock Alley after the economic slump of the late 1980s, I found myself doing whatever I could for creative inspiration—studying books, getting out to visit with supportive customers, and attending the major textile shows in Frankfurt and Paris, as well as the home furnishings shows in New York and High Point, N.C.

How I managed to do any of this with my head held high I don't know, since both my psyche and Peacock Alley's financial situation had taken a major hit. We were operating on such a shoestring then. Money was coming in slower, which made it go out slower. I sweated numerous Fridays, worrying about having enough money to meet payroll. And somehow I found the strength to place orders with suppliers whom I already owed money. I simply chose to be honest about Peacock Alley's financial limitations—which I explained would be temporary, since we had a new banking agreement—and they in return would cut me a bit of slack.

Such a scenario seems so unlikely in this day and age, but we had built up a strong relationship and trust level. I say this because it underscores the true benefit of relationship building, which my family and I have always valued. We worked to earn business on many levels, staying in tune with our clients' needs, expressing real empathy for their professional and personal situations, helping them acquire new business whenever possible, sharing whatever insight might be relevant. That's still our mantra. Luxurious bedding was appearing to be a beacon for our future, which indicated to me that Peacock Alley should focus more on the quality of what was under the cover instead of just what was on it. Sales of the sumptuous Italian sheeting were far exceeding our expectations, and my hunch had been right: Once people experienced Egyptian cotton, with its crisp, cool, marvelously soft texture, they were sold on what a difference it could make in their lives.

What also was becoming clear was Peacock Alley's strong suit: A curated look, with sheeting in mostly whites, beiges, taupes or soft neutrals, in mainly solids, but occasionally with stripes, Swiss dot, soft jacquard or plaid—just enough to be interesting without being distracting. But in terms of offerings, I was really at the mercy of our suppliers, leaving me hard-pressed to find colors and patterns not being picked up on by competitors or larger retailers.

Could I have had 24 colors of sheeting? Yes, but that wasn't the point. I wanted what I believed to be the smartest choices of the (neutral) lot. At the time, such thinking went against the grain. Most of our competitors were building their success on fleeting fashion trends. I wanted Peacock Alley to always be in style, to be what one might call "the little black dress" of bedding—basics with which a "wardrobe" of linens could be built. It wasn't time- or cost-effective to build each bedding ensemble from the ground up. If we wanted a new coverlet, for instance, chances of bringing it into the fold were higher if we already had sheets to pair with it. My goal was also to be surrounded by people who could constantly question whether a potential product would fit into our wardrobe.

Commitment to what already was adding volume to our sales was always popular with some of our sales team, who thought we should stay on top of the trends. Ray and I even had our moments over this issue. As he once told a reporter, "She has her classic look, and no one's going to convince her that another look should be under the Peacock Alley umbrella. I know, because I tried."

Well, I'd gotten this far in life by taking risks, and actually, staying true to a more elegant, classic look was one of them. Such a timeless style

PAGE 146) Our national advertising campaign extended to our bath line in this concept shot from the mid-1990s. We loved the feel of "going under cover."

LEFT) Peacock Alley is most known for its iconic, crisp white bedding— our Serenade coverlet, bedskirt and shams were always a favorite. In fact, this product was featured in Neiman Marcus' catalog in much the same way.

seemed a novel and sustainable concept in the age of excess. (And if I did consider straying, I always asked myself, what's the downside risk and the upside potential of doing so.)

To my mind, more is not more: Opulent old-world embellishments have their place, but they can lean more toward ostentatious than classic if not kept in check. Besides maintaining good client relationships, we also had an underlying passion for developing the highest quality product at the best price. We listened intently to our clients to learn what their customers really needed and wanted to serve their needs. But all of these efforts were becoming more difficult as competitors were watching, and increasingly copying, our every move.

By the mid-1990s, the larger retail stores had their eyes on Peacock Alley. At the decade's end they would venture away from offering only the inexpensive variety of mid-quality cottons and instead try to buy into the upscale market with "hotel"-branded sheeting. We, of course, already had entered that market in terms of what we were offering; we just didn't start branding it as such until later on, and only when we felt the product really matched up to the name.

The major stores foray into "high style" sheeting did cut into our market but at the same time actually helped us by raising consumer awareness of better bedding. I knew that once their customers made the step to improve their bedding they'd experience a step up in quality—but then wonder what else was out there. How might they move their bedding a few notches up the chain without having to spend a solid fortune?

To stay ahead of the game, we'd need to have more control over our offerings, and one way to do that would be to somehow "own" the European look—to be guaranteed we had exactly what we were envisioning. Ray, of course, had an idea. He held the key to another financial saving grace, one that would be right under our feet.

As our family farm took shape, so did Ray's interest in living off the land, not merely on it. Its sandy loam soil had once been part of the Brazos River, making it excellent for drainage and ideal for planting. That would prove a small boon.

Ray and I loved good food—lightly prepared and beautifully seasoned—and especially enjoyed dining out when traveling on business. The tough financial years of the late '80s and early '90s took a toll on how often we could travel together, so that left us dining more often closer to home, which wasn't too disappointing. The "New American" food revolution's heralded Southwest cuisine craze had made Dallas one of the most exciting places to be outside of Santa Fe, thanks to such inventive, now legendary, chefs as Dean Fearing, then at The Mansion on Turtle Creek, and Stephen Pyles, of Routh Street Cafe.

Ray was decidedly a raconteur but he also was a keen observer and listener. He chatted with the chefs after each meal, often inquiring about the

LEFT) Josh and Meredith riding bikes at the farm in Granbury, with their dogs Miller and Mason, from a story that appeared in *Better Homes & Gardens*.

unique foods they really wanted to get but couldn't—or at least couldn't get as fresh as they would have liked.

As Ray was inspired to plant those unusual foods (and inventively cook with them), I could see his marketing wheels turning. He aimed to help us keep the farm by putting it to work.

When I think back to that time, I remember warm, breezy evenings, and heavenly wafts of the herbs that first graced our garden. Soon came fancy lettuces, then baby vegetables. Ray was in constant communication with his culinary clients, letting them know the status of their crops. And those chefs knew a good thing when they saw it (and tasted it). Gabler Farm fare could be from farm to table in just hours after being cut.

We planted other fancy greens, beets, eight different types of basil, sorrel, baby leeks and garlic, and heirloom produce—most of it commissioned by the chefs. All of this was grown organically, with Ray light years ahead of mainstream acceptance of such old-school farming techniques.

As one of the first pioneers of the slow food movement, Ray's excitement and enthusiasm was infectious. He couldn't wait to show some chef his new crop of something-or-other. With two full-time businesses operating outside the farm, the pace for both of us was beyond hectic. There was a lot of going and coming from our farm during those days. And I laugh to think about some of our neighbors, who wondered if some of what we were growing was illegal.

Ray marketed his foods not only to the top chefs, but also to such retail outlets as Paula Lambert's Mozzarella Cheese Co., and a purveyor of frozen Italian foods—which once ordered 2,000 basil plants; with that order Ray knew he'd made it.

Our worries about maintaining the farm and both our businesses were supplanted by a thriving garden, one that grew from the small plot near the house to three acres of crops staggered seasonally. That ensured a continual harvest, and also helped us meet living expenses.

Ray's ingenuity was brilliant on many levels. He used every bit of that land. He planted marigolds and nasturtiums around the garden as natural insect repellents, but they, too, were edible and sellable. He not only sold Texas wild mustang grapes but also their vines, flavorful for use in grilling. He dried the needles from surrounding cedar trees to make into sachets. And with always-abundant cucumbers and garlic, he made his own garlic pickles he sold at gourmet shops and restaurants.

None of this work made a great deal of money as much as it was a way to survive the economic downturn in a fulfilling way. I wasn't surprised Gabler Farm became a viable side business. Ray's products were good, there was no doubt about that. But his personality made them even better. He was so good at cultivating relationships as well as food.

When I look back at that time I'm deeply touched by what he did to help us survive, all while running his other business and helping me with mine. And he did it with such passion, which always helps grow a business. It's so important to do what makes you happy; success will follow. I can attest to that.

For years to come, both of us would be happiest in the garden near our home, working quietly on the weekends, feeling contented in each other's presence. After a good physical day's work we'd sit on our porch, sip a julep infused with just-picked mint, and look out at our handiwork. We'd talk about ideas to pursue in the weeks to come, and while doing so, enjoy watching our longhorn "couple" grazing in the distance. Those were some of the few precious (quiet) moments during that time.

As the economy improved, orders were coming in from every direction for both his businesses, and Ray stood at a crossroads. Either he was going to give Gabler Farm his full-time focus or he would need to put that energy into his existing business. Wisely, he chose the latter, but took pride

MATELASSÉ: THE FRENCH CONNECTION

Peacock Alley is recognized for having popularized matelassé bedding in the U.S. That, of course, gives me a warm, cozy feeling, just like the classic, embossed-style coverlet itself.

Matelassé, French for "quilted" or "cushioned" textile, in its modern guise is meant to mimic the style of hand-stitched 18th-century quilts made in the south of France.

As a devotee of heirloom linens, I'd long admired matelassé for several reasons. The lightweight yet thick cotton coverlets offer simple yet dressy top-of-bed fashion that's durable and easy-care. They're woven in a triple weave, resulting in a raised pattern with a slightly puffed, "quilted" look. And they're most often found in white or ecru, two of my favorite colors. I'd kept an eye out for vintage matelassé whenever traveling in France or Italy. Realizing how scarce those quilts were, it occurred to me that we should update them and feature them as part of the Peacock Alley line.

Our matelassé fabrics, made of 100-percent Egyptian cotton, or cotton linen blends, are woven on jacquard looms in Portugal and Italy.

Here are three favorites:
Vienna, Peacock Alley's signature matelassé for more than 30 years, features understated curves inspired by an antique button found in France.

Alyssa is finely crafted with eight rows of double-needle stitching, applied on a sophisticated diamond design.

Montauk may be the perfect modern neutral for the sophisticated bed, with a luxe allover pebble pattern in fresh white, soft pearl or natural linen hues, double-row details and an engineered frame border.

OPPOSITE) Ray is pictured with
a harvest from his garden at the
farm. We had about 30 acres
of coastal bermuda, which we
had baled.

in the fact he'd fulfilled a dream. I will always be grateful for what he did to sustain us in troubled times, to help feed others and nurture many creative spirits.

For style and quality consistency, Ray and I knew we'd need to partner with various European mills. We also knew that wouldn't be easy. Most of them had decades, if not a century or two, perfecting their fine linens, and might take offense at our offering input into their production— asking, for instance, for a better finish, or dictating a certain design detail, such as a 4-inch top-sheet cuff—and all completed to U.S. bedding specifications. These mills, however, wanted a piece of the growing U.S. market.

In 1988, a little Portuguese mill would change not only our minds about any potential ego sparring, but also our business model. And while the mill was old-school in technique, it was modern-minded enough to play ball with us. Making inroads into the U.S. was more alluring for them after American mills began closing in the Carolinas and moving to Asia.

They not only offered sumptuous textiles, but their price points were less than the ones in Italy; Portugal had lower labor costs, which would allow us a better profit. By our working together, the mill could obtain and grow a market they wanted and in turn help us maintain and grow our own market.

Thus, we had the opportunity to be one of the first U.S. purveyors of Portuguese luxury sheeting. The only thing stopping us was capital. Ray and I turned to one of his former Wamsutta colleagues to help us fund our first couple of containers of textiles and introduce them to the market. Their immediately positive reception allowed us to pay Ray's former colleague back and in turn, invest in more product.

It was thrilling to be able to take European sheeting in the direction we'd always wanted. Portuguese sheeting offered an incredible sleeping experience, especially after we helped them finesse the sheeting to our

LEFT) Here I am gathering lettuces and herbs from Morning Glory Farms on Martha's Vineyard, where we buy our vegetables when we're in town.

specifications. The adaptations put them more on par with our Italian linens, which we continued to carry.

We branded our collaborative product as Peacock Alley sheets made in Portugal. And we gave those early sheets musical names—Soprano, Solo, Duet, Lyric and Virtuoso—to reflect the upbeat, joyful experience we had at the time. Most of these sheets are still in our line today.

Specialty stores and major department stores gobbled up the product with gusto, which we had hoped they would. It was, as we said at the time, a win-win: Stores carrying our products would profit financially, and distinguish themselves from competitors.

"Peacock Alley meets or beats the more costly foreign competition," Jackson, Miss., boutique owner Ray Reinhardt told *The Dallas Morning News*. "If you're an independent, you need a Peacock Alley kind of line that's upscale yet value priced. You can't sell popular-priced linen because the department stores have that market covered up."

As enthusiasm was building, along with double-digit growth, the weight was lifting. More money was coming in, along with raves for our Peacock Alley products. The luxury bedding business was growing as well—use of linen, for example, grew as much as 25 percent from '93 to '95, with consumers willing to pay more money than ever for bedding.

More demand meant more product and a larger staff to ensure it. Our confidence grew as well. Then came our unique national black and white advertising campaign that positioned us not just as a bedding company, but also as a lifestyle, doing the unexpected in a tasteful way that piqued the consumers' curiosity.

In 1996, my son Josh, fresh from the University of Miami, told me he wanted to join Peacock Alley and start selling. While I admired that, and did ultimately want his help, my main hesitation in saying yes was that as his mother, I didn't want to be his first boss. I could tell he was a natural salesman, but I wanted him to first prove himself in a bigger company and then, armed with more discipline and experience, be better equipped to join us.

Josh was determined to prove me wrong. As somewhat of a wild horse, he wouldn't make things easy. But he would make things interesting. He reminds me with that bright smile of his that I "hired him and fired him several times." This is true. I put him in customer service to get his feet wet, but it was obvious I was going to have to get him on the road, where, in sales-measurable ways, he could work out his playful, even prankster, spirit. (He once tripped the fire alarm so a colleague could run an errand.)

By the next year, with Peacock Alley's growth being nothing short of spectacular, Ray had sold his business and joined ours as executive vice president. He wanted his first order of business to be taking Josh under his wing. That would be interesting. When that duo got together they were like two little boys. (I loved seeing the bond between them; it dovetailed nicely with the sales and marketing mentorship Josh received from his father, Michael.) When tasked with handling Peacock Alley's Midwest sales territory, however, Josh hunkered down and got serious.

Unbeknownst to Josh, that resistant-to-change region was our toughest market. That would be even more so for a sales newbie. The tepid reception Josh received just made him work harder. He turned on his Southern charm, which reflected his fun-loving yet caring attitude. It wasn't long before orders picked up there, surprising us all—so much so that Ray ultimately put him in charge of the even-more-promising Southern California territory. Josh had proven me wrong—and Peacock Alley very right.

About the same time we hired Josh, we also hired Krista Sonnier, a former professional ballerina. While she had little retail experience, what Ray and I could really see in her was a passion for the luxury bedding

business. That to us made all the difference between her and a more seasoned professional. We put her in charge of our burgeoning outlet, where she quadrupled sales, raking in $1.25 million three years in a row. (Again, hire people who love what they do and success will follow.)

In the meantime we opened our first flagship retail store in Dallas. The building, a former rectory-turned-window company, was filled with beautiful natural light. Before long, it was filled with customers.

By the end of the 1990s, we were a growing, $20-million company. We had claimed significant footing in brand awareness, had in operation a 26,000-square-foot production plant and a team of very focused and dedicated people. In 1999, the prestigious Caruth Institute for Entrepreneurship at SMU's Cox School of Business named us one of the "100 Fastest-Growing Companies" in Dallas, and for two years we made *Inc.* magazine's 500 list. I'd been also nominated for Ernst & Young's "Entrepreneur of the Year." My sons were thriving—Josh was doing very well in the company and Jason was now a sales leader at the video game manufacturer Activision. Each also had gotten married.

I didn't think life could be any rosier.

"Martha Stewart may have Kmart but Mary Ella Gabler has Neiman Marcus, Horchow and London's Fortnum & Mason" a newspaper once reported. We also had Harrod's of London, Saks Fifth Avenue, Macy's and Bloomingdale's. By Y2K we had 800 retailers and catalogue companies in this country and abroad that had gotten on board with our products.

To celebrate, Ray and I purchased a pre-war condo in Manhattan's Sutton Place neighborhood, fulfilling the dream I'd had since leaving the city in the '60s to one day return — as a success. The pied-à-terre, painted a frightful shade of '50s avocado green, was another "re-do" opportunity for us, one that this time would offer me a decidedly less rustic design canvas.

The New York investment also inspired Peacock Alley's first store outside of Dallas, in this case, only blocks away from our apartment. I could see the basic structure would make a beautiful linen store. And it did. Its gorgeous back patio made a lovely place to host tea and cocktail mixers—yet another sales and marketing opportunity that helped make us the toast of lifestyle bedding design.

We also had begun an innovative program to open Peacock Alley Boutiques in what would be total of 28 stores.

Ray and I were living the dream. But we were doing so, it seems, in a house of cards. When you are financed to the hilt, anything's possible. Until it all comes crashing down.

PAGE 170) Josh and Lake at
M.L. Leddy's, the custom
boot maker in Fort Worth.
We started going there when
Josh's dad was alive, and we
still give them as gifts. I have
several pairs—I love wearing
my boots in the winter with
almost any of my clothes;
They fit like no other.
OPPOSITE) Peacock Alley's
Chevron bathrobe and towels
are 100 percent Egyptian
cotton made in Portugal.

LEFT) This Madeleine
matelassé, introduced
in 2008, was a sleek,
modern departure from
our traditional look,
in new toned neutrals of
shell and bronze.

BRAND-NEW APPROACH

Buoyed by the success of our Portuguese bedding, in 1995 we decided the time was right to launch a national advertising campaign. With limited investment dollars, however, we'd have to get especially creative. We'd also need to find just the right person to lead us in that direction. We accomplished both goals by turning to creative director Kristin Atwell of Atwell Design, who shortly beforehand had created some interesting visuals for our linens packaging. I really liked her style, both professional and personal.

Newly divorced, the forward-thinker had just moved into a small home, which was full of stacked boxes. We met across the surface of her impromptu conference table—a grand piano. (What a clever use of space!) I was immediately impressed by her creative, forge-ahead outlook on life. We instantly bonded.

After reviewing our budget, then the cost to advertise in magazines popular with our clientele (*House & Garden, Elle Decor, Southern Accents*), Kristin decided we shouldn't have to choose one publication over the other. If we went with full-page black-and-white displays, we could advertise in all of them. But how could we possibly make bedding look good in a colorless context?

Kristin wasn't deterred by such a challenge; in fact, she was inspired by it. Black and white photography could allow us to do something edgy, something ethereal and hip, something that could set us apart from most bedding companies, which were simply showing beds looking prim and perfect.

Our task would be to project a memorable, powerful look and message that would set us apart from others in the industry. Each ad should have a quirky, avant-garde spirit, one exuding confidence and sophistication.

We'd take our cues from fashion, inspired by what powerhouses like Prada were doing with provocative ads that raised eyebrows—and brand awareness. No other home fashion company was taking such an approach. Here was our chance.

We dreamed up surreal concepts: A girl floating over a bed, beckoning us to "Rise Above It All." A model in an inviting floral bed, hair styled to look like a flower, advising us to "Bloom Where You Are Planted." A tousled bed implying something adventurous had just taken place there.

"It was unusual, that's for sure. And it didn't always go over well with everyone," Kristin recalls. "We definitely pushed people past their comfort zones."

I must admit, at times I was one of them. It wasn't because I didn't like the ads; it was mostly because some of our devoted customers had told me they missed us showing how to beautifully dress a bed. To them, our new look was nothing short of "messy."

Ray, however, urged me on; so did our then-creative director (and Jason's wife) Leslie Needleman. Without a doubt, the effort and gamble was worth it. Each time *House & Garden* ran one of the ads, readers sent in cards requesting information in record numbers. *H&G* was floored. We were too.

We maintained that edgy advertising style for a number of years, with new themes and stunning photography. Those ads are remembered by our customers even 20 years after they were introduced. And they seem as fresh as ever.

Our national advertising campaign featured dramatic black-and-white concept shots. Each was punctuated with jaunty quips I loved. These are still a few of my favorites. **OPPOSITE)** "Create an uplifting environment and rise above it all." **ABOVE)** "Bloom where you are planted. It's all about cultivating the bed." **RIGHT)** "For maximum personal growth, sprinkle daily with tranquility."

FOR MAXIMUM PERSONAL GROWTH,
SPRINKLE DAILY WITH TRANQUILITY.

Peacock Alley

If you're in a bad situation, don't worry, it'll change. If you're in a good situation, don't worry, it'll change.

—JOHN A. SIMONE, SR.

Optimists like me never imagine the worst. So when the worst does happen, the punch is especially hard, especially when family takes the hit, too.

Such was the case in 2003, as Ray and I sat together in a Dallas office hearing the coldly delivered news that Peacock Alley was coming apart at the seams. The banks were doing what they'd done nearly 20 years before: calling in their loans to the tune of nearly everything we owned.

How could this be happening—again?

We had been riding high for 10 years. The economy was healthy. Our customer base was growing, as was our revenue, much of which was invested back into the company to fund projects promising even greater returns. With growth a constant, I wasn't worried by all of the expenses incurred while juggling new retail endeavors, our branding campaign, the New York apartment needs, increased travel, new hires and the constant financing of containers arriving from Europe.

Then came the devastation of 9/11, when the terror attacks caused the economy to grind to a stop in 2001. And with that, the luxury-goods market didn't just soften, it declined quickly. When banks became nervous about their marginally profitable commercial accounts, what followed was an audit of Peacock Alley, one that would shake the ground beneath us. As Ray and I learned the extent of our troubles, the banks called in a "workout plan" specialist. I called in my son Jason.

"Remember, this was right after the Enron scandal, the biggest audit failure in history," he recalled. "All corporations were under microscopes."

I trusted Jason could offer a fresh perspective on what we faced. Like me, he had sales and marketing in his blood, but he had a greater propensity for numbers. That was apparent from his success at Activision, which he had helped grow from a $33 million company into a billion-dollar powerhouse. My request for his help, however, couldn't have come at a worse time. Within the past year he and Josh had lost their father, Michael, whose sudden death needed a painful sorting out. Peacock Alley's financial failings were the last thing I wanted them to worry about, but it was what it was.

Jason didn't get the full measure of what we were facing until reviewing our balance sheets and income statements. The books were unusual in how they were set up to recognize revenue, making it appear that Peacock Alley had a lot more collateral than it really had. The banks had been loaning against those optimistic numbers, and Peacock Alley was mere weeks away from bankruptcy. The news was a staggering surprise. Ray and I felt so foolish. Our eyes had been firmly fixed on sales, marketing and innovation. We had trusted others to tend to the company's financials, but that led to our ship running aground as we borrowed as much as we felt we needed, paid off the debt, then borrowed more on numbers that turned out to be inaccurate.

We would need new financial managment, certainly, but that wasn't any of the banks' concern. They just wanted their money. And who could blame them? Things had gotten out of control. We had massive asset and branding opportunity losses, and our pride took a hit.

The biggest hurt for Ray was the failure of our Peacock Alley Boutiques. Several years earlier, he had developed the Boutiques concept to leverage to the max our sales and marketing. Realizing inventory is much better on others' shelves than our own, the plan was to install bedding and lifestyle vignettes inside the stores of our most successful retailers. We would handle the expense of that, along with merchandising, styling and sales and marketing training. The retailer's responsibility was to maintain our look, promote each Boutique, and each week pay for what had been sold.

PAGE 180) Byron was Peacock Alley's first cotton linen floral matelassé from Italy.
ABOVE) Josh Needleman, vice president of business development for Peacock Alley.
LEFT) Jason Needleman, CEO of Peacock Alley. These were shot at our loft in Fort Worth at a family dinner. Jason and Josh are so different. Josh is the free spirit who talks to everybody, knows everybody and is sales and marketing oriented. Jason does things in such a quiet way, but he's very strong. He has exceptional talents.

The collaboration was perfect in that we were ensured greater sales, while the stores minimized their investment risk. We were delighted with the results. Within two years, sales of our product in the Boutiques, in 28 stores, had doubled and in some cases tripled.

The Boutiques were a hit, but the economic slump had sealed their fate. The banks demanded that the $1.5 million worth of our inventory in the marketplace be returned to our warehouse immediately to repay our loans.

This, of course, spelled disaster for not only us but our top retailers. Before initiating the Boutiques program we had gone to great lengths to prove the concept would work. Now we had to pull the rug out from under everyone and bring all the merchandise back to Peacock Alley—and still hope for good working relationships. It was a costly, time-consuming, logistical mess, but thankfully because of Ray's and Josh's efforts to honestly explain the situation, we lost only one retailer.

Making matters worse were my own monetary losses. The stock I'd inherited from my late mother, pledged against our loans, was as good as gone. That was traumatic for several reasons, none bigger than the money had been my mother's security in her later years. After my father's passing it had helped her gain the self-confidence she'd long craved after a controlling marriage. Now here I was, having it all disappear in seemingly careless fashion. But I knew my mother had been proud of what I had accomplished, and deep down I believed she would have supported my giving up everything to save Peacock Alley—and in essence, our family's livelihood—and start anew.

Another blow was the brow beating I took from the financial advisors and attorneys handling financial mismanagement. How, a few asked, could I have let Peacock Alley get into such a state? And why was I involving Jason, who was inexperienced in corporate turnarounds?

LEFT) Here I am with my granddaughters Lucy Ray and Mary Eloise having one of our tickle sessions on the bed in our loft in Fort Worth. **PAGE 191)** Peacock Alley's Soprano sheeting, in 400 thread count cotton sateen, was introduced in the early 1990s and is still our best-selling sheet.

I didn't know the answer to the first question; that would take a while. I did know the answer to the second: Quite simply, he was my son, and in difficult times, you turn to family. There's no explaining that, really. A family does what's needed to survive. That was instilled in me long ago.

All of Peacock Alley's problems, mine especially, affected Ray. Emotionally he was a wreck over the situation. He had worked so hard to create a program that, in hindsight, could have succeeded had we paid more attention to the numbers. Although it was my collateral that was lost, not his, I know how badly he felt. We tried not to talk about it a lot. We just vowed to work harder than ever to get past it.

While Josh, Ray and I kept Peacock Alley moving forward on the sales front, Jason spent a year and a half helping us to gain a clearer financial picture and better accounting system. Major input came from a corporate turnaround specialist who coached Jason behind the scenes as he talked the banks into giving us one last chance. The result was a lifesaver: Instead of having to pay back the banks immediately, they gave us a rigid, 12-month workout plan. It would be an enormous task, but with financial help from Jason and Josh—who later became major shareholders in Peacock Alley—we not only met the plan's terms, but did so in 10 months.

Working alongside Jason to make this happen was Paul Hamilton, one of the many self-made people in our company. Paul moved to the U.S. from South Africa in the early 1990s and joined us in the warehouse to help pay his way through college. As he studied for his accounting degree, his financial-support role and commitment to seeing us succeed would ultimately pay off. Paul, today our vice president of finance, demonstrated his dedication and upstanding character, the most important traits of any employee. Skills can be taught. Passion, and the ability to earn trust, can't.

Jason's wife Leslie and I kept the creative fires lit while my family, including my extended family at Peacock Alley, worked diligently to keep negativity from spreading like wildfire. All of us felt so responsible for each other's well being and livelihood.

Our biggest naysayers were our competitors, who were more than happy to tell customers that Peacock Alley's loss of retail counter space and reduced staff signaled our demise. But fortunately, almost without exception, our loyal clients, with whom we'd built solid relationships, just weren't buying it. They were sticking with us, and that in itself was priceless. This showed we had not only a quality product but a quality business.

Jason, positive throughout, said of that difficult restructuring, "I practically earned an MBA because of it." With an appetite whet for other corporate challenges, he returned to video animation work. Though I understood why—it was his first love–I secretly hoped he would rejoin Peacock Alley. Having both of my sons at my side had been personally and professionally fulfilling.

When all was said and done, Ray and I could see in black and white (and red) that as our business structure became more complex, we just didn't have the financial vision to handle it. That part of the business had been secondary; creating beautiful products and building our brand was first and foremost. The thrill of success had been too intoxicating, the details of somehow paying the bills for all of it overlooked. Problems, though, will not go away if simply ignored. I had to lose nearly all I was worth, twice, to understand that.

Peacock Alley's financials would need to be placed in the hands of people with more expertise, and people we could deeply trust. We would need to operate as debt-free as possible. And before any growth opportunities were embraced, no matter their seeming viability, we'd need to bank on more than just positive thinking. Did we have the staffing, the technology, the necessary savings to weather an economic storm?

What successes might we have had if we had been more wise about things? That's something I try not to think about. That's the optimist in me. But I do know this: Life as a roller coaster ride had been thrilling. Being on the brink of insolvency had not.

Our rebuilding years did see new successes. National magazines such as *House Beautiful* and *Traditional Home* recognized our cache by featuring us in photo shoots. We also heard more about our celebrity fans. Our bedding could be found in celebrities' homes from Sag Harbor to Los Angeles and St. Bart's. We also had been the official bedding for Pope John Paul II during a visit, thanks largely to St. Louis' Sallie Home, one of our longtime retailers.

Positivity, which helped lift us during the bleak years, came from our customers as well as our team members, who continue to be true ambassadors for Peacock Alley. Dale Cooper is among them.

Dale is a champion in times of strife. Her late husband, David, had worked with Ray at Wamsutta and later was one of the first to introduce Egyptian cotton towels to the U.S. When David died unexpectedly while running a marathon in San Francisco, Ray and I were touched that Dale, then a young mother and nurse-turned-real estate agent, did her best to keep their family business going. "I had no choice but to quickly learn the ropes," Dale said. "My family's survival was counting on it."

Greatly impressed by Dale's devotion, Ray continually tried to entice her to come work with us: "Why don't you come on over to the right side of the fence?" he'd say with a big smile. "It's nice over here." One day his charm worked, and she joined forces with Peacock Alley. Dale's caring and determination have been a great source of strength for us in so many sales areas, including catalog, hospitality and wholesale.

I'm also reminded of some stress relievers during those trying years. Once, after a gift show in New York, I thought it would be great fun for

some of us to pay a visit to my old hangout, Marie's Crisis Cafe in Greenwich Village. "After a long day and a few martinis, we discovered we were the only women there," Krista Sonnier recalled. "Needless to say, we ordered more martinis. An unemployed Broadway performer was belting out show tunes at the piano, and soon we were singing along with everyone in the bar, into the wee hours of the morning." (Oh, how my head hurt the next day.)

On the home front, Ray and I counted our many blessings. By then they included grandchildren Grant and Lake, born in 2001, Elise and Cole in 2003, and Lucy Ray in 2004. Eloise would follow in 2007. To them I am "Gigi," which definitely beats "Grandma Gabler." They brought much-needed joy to our lives during troubled times, which definitely put things in proper perspective.

The new generation of Needlemans also influenced Peacock Alley's product line. With the grandchildren in mind, we began designing sumptuous bedding for babies, then children and teens, all with a mid-century modern influence. Their positive reception indicated that others were enjoying our ebullience, as if we were one big family. Inclusion of our customers as a part of our extended family is something we continue to promote.

Ray and I were proud that Josh was growing our business in innovative ways while his wife Meredith was excelling in customer service. Leslie was helping design all of the coordinates that went into each bedding ensemble and helping us win raves. My daughters-in-law are each very talented individuals, and with a united front, we made a strong team.

It had been an intense few years but it appeared the worst was behind us. Peacock Alley was back on track, with product success and customer loyalty stronger than ever.

During the test of our will and stamina, Ray and I found great comfort at the farm, cooking and gardening together as Patsy Cline or George Jones crooned in the background. But it was obvious Ray was a changed man, emotionally and physically. His inner light had dimmed, and everyone who knew him noticed. His attentiveness wasn't quite what it had been, his complexion paler, his bearing less confident. His exuberant self would at times reappear, as when dinner party conversations turned to politics, and his pontifications, fueled by too much wine, left me no choice but to give him a kick to the shin underneath the table.

Ray's health began to deteriorate in 2006. Then one afternoon at the farm I found him slumped over the wheel of his ATV. The left side of his body was numb, he told me. I drove him as fast as I could to an emergency room, where we learned he'd need immediate quadruple bypass heart surgery. After that, as he grew even weaker, a massive stroke led to hospice care. None of us could believe this larger-than-life man, such a force of creativity and positivity, was slipping away from us, right before our eyes.

As *Home Textiles Today* wrote, "Raymond F. Gabler, 78, a courtly Texas tastemaker and marketer, the husband of Mary Ella Gabler, founder of Peacock Alley, died Sept. 22 at West Community Hospice with his wife at his side. A tall distinguished looking Texan with a gift for political repartee and a flair for home fashions, Gabler had been vice president of marketing for Peacock Alley, the carriage-trade resource founded by his wife of 26 years."

Ray's death left a huge void in all of our lives. "He laid down an amazing foundation," said Krista, whom he saw as his second daughter. "He truly believed in the power of Peacock Alley, and he believed in all of us. His pride in what we as a team, we as a family, were creating, selling and branding was immense. All who knew and loved him will continue that legacy."

RAY'S QUILT

The box had arrived. Knowing the value of its contents, I carefully guided a letter opener down the center seam until an opening brought forth an unexpected gift: the strong smell of kerosene. The acrid scent was one I'd known during my earliest days inside Pennsylvania Dutch farmhouses, ones much like the source of this package. Inside the box were two quilts Amish women had made from two dozen of Ray's favorite shirts. I'd seen a memory quilt created with old ties, so why not? And besides, I couldn't bear to part with his shirts. Ray had taken such pride in them, and had looked so dapper ("jaunty" even, a journalist wrote).

In two years' time, the shirts' crisp colors and smart patterns had been skillfully combined into a kaleidoscope of small, geometrically arranged squares, resulting in two of the most amazing new quilts I'd seen.

Since the makers of the quilts eschewed electricity and telephones in living the simple life, contacting them hadn't been easy. So I'd asked a cousin in my hometown of Chambersburg, Pa., to drive the shirts and backing fabric to them, about an hour north into the mountains. She made contact with the ladies, told them Ray's story, and shared with them the ideas I had for the quilt pattern.

Stitched by the light and warmth of the hearth, their work far exceeded what I'd imagined. Their efforts produced true treasures.

One quilt went to Josh, whose close connection with Ray had been obvious. The other went to Ray's granddaughter when she married. And what a beautiful feeling that was. I never thought I'd see my way toward brighter days, but I did. Ray, always the positive thinker, would have insisted.

LEFT) The lovely
fashion bedding line
Lotus, released in 2009,
always evoked the
simple botanical feel
of the farm to me with
its detailed embroidery
and soft monochromatic
palette. Pure solace.
And extraordinarily
beautiful.

A memorial service for Ray was held at the farm, and afterward his ashes were spread in the garden. I knew he would want to rest there, commingled with the crops we'd cherished.

A few months later, after I was able to stay at the farm by myself, I experienced a moment that will stay with me forever.

From the screened porch I could see them: slender, green stalks in the garden, vibrant additions to a late-fall landscape. Our spring asparagus was making a fall debut, as it had before, much to Ray's delight. I caught myself wanting to tell him. But something told me he already knew.

OPPOSITE) Our farm is filled with big oaks, old pecans, persimmon trees and cedars. Here, Ray and I are walking with Jason's son Grant at age 4, at the entrance to the farm in Granbury.

THREADS THAT COUNT

The our-thread-count-is-higher-than-yours craze prompted unscrupulous manufacturers to split yarns in order to call them two instead of one, upping their purported thread count and making it possible to sell "luxury" sheets at unbelievable prices (while compromising integrity).

Peacock Alley never joined in such games, but eventually we were forced to emphasize thread count on our packaging. Fortunately the trend seems to be righting itself, with most major bedding suppliers no longer promoting thread counts. If the marketing ploy accomplished anything, it was to help make people more aware of what they were buying. What really matters is the type of yarn that's spun.

Egyptian cotton is white gold in our business. It's the highest-quality, longest-staple cotton available. It's twice as thick as most cottons and supremely soft, making it stronger, more lustrous, more luxurious. The main thing to know is there's a limit to the number of threads you can ideally have in a square inch of fabric—at the very best, 500 or 600. Yes, 1,000 is possible, but the result is a very thick fabric, the antithesis of supple, luxury bedding.

Also important is how the textile feels. Many prefer percale sheeting, with its tight, basket-weave styling that provides a crisp touch and fluffy appearance, and is especially nice in summer. Others favor sateen, which has a lengthwise weave that reflects light, and results in a glossy, satiny look and cozier feel.

Whatever your choice, remember true quality will stand the test of time.

Feelings of worth can flourish only in an atmosphere where individual differences are appreciated, mistakes are tolerated, communication is open, and rules are flexible— the kind of atmosphere that is found in a nurturing family.

—VIRGINIA SATIR

After five emotion-wrought years, channeling my energy into Peacock Alley may have been a form of escape, but it did offer a sense of lightness. I traveled more, seeking design inspiration everywhere—from the lacy webs of winter tree branches to the wavy textures of beach sand. I strengthened myself physically through golf and tennis, and spiritually in the comfort of books, art and the people I love. Staying busy left no time to become mired in depression. Everyone agreed on that. I also was adjusting to life without a mate, but two close friends wanted that to change. In the fall of 2007, Jerry and Emy Lou Baldridge were determined that I meet John F. Bitzer, Jr.

Like me, John was a dear friend Emy Lou had known for decades. John also had lost a longtime spouse, Mimi, to whom he was married for 45 years. And, like me, he had strong ties to Pennsylvania: He was living in Pittsburgh as the recently retired CEO of ABARTA, a family-owned holding company involved in publishing, food and beverage sales, and oil and gas exploration. John and I had actually met once five years earlier during a group trip to Ireland; we'd even sat next to each other at a dinner.

As I thumbed through a photo album looking for proof, I did remember the sumptuous Irish manor house we'd all stayed in, and the country's amazing scenery. Emy Lou pointed to a picture of a white-haired gentleman with chiseled features. Oh, yes, I did remember John—specifically, his large horn-rimmed glasses, which weren't the best look for him, I recalled thinking. I then remembered a conversation we had about strategic planning, one Emy Lou had deliberately encouraged us to have, knowing I was heavily into it then. But the chat hadn't been as enlightening as it had been intimidating, so I was rather underwhelmed by the prospect of another meeting.

Emy Lou and Jerry insisted we reconnect, however, so I agreed to a trip

PAGE 202) I use our outdoor shower at Martha's Vineyard all the time. Everyone who stays in the house says it's their favorite shower. It's a wonderful thing to bathe outdoors—we have an outside shower at the Granbury farm too. The robe and towels are Peacock Alley's waffle weave. **RIGHT AND BELOW)** John and I enjoying a family gathering at the loft. Santa Fe artist Marcia Myers did the painting in the background. It was made in three different pieces and put together. I hung it on a sliding wall that separates our office from the dining room.

to Martha's Vineyard. I'd play along, if only to see the island, which I'd never seen. Besides, since John had his own home there, if we didn't click he could easily retreat without much awkwardness. The Baldridges and a few other couples had spent the weekend there, having made their yearly trip to the Vineyard. Over the years, they had also named themselves "The Society of a Friend or Two." I had met a few of these people in previous years and was eager to reconnect. I had also heard that the 1915 poem by Wilbur Nesbit, "A Friend or Two" was always read by Jerry before dinners at the home. How sweet.

While John told Emy Lou he did remember me, it was obvious upon meeting again that he expected someone else—another blonde who'd been on the Ireland trip. Jerry reminds everyone to this day that John looked palpably relieved. We had a good laugh, though, and went with the flow.

As Emy Lou and Jerry feted us, John revealed himself to be a reserved, genteel and scholarly New Englander. Born in Hartford, Conn., he is an

LEFT) John at Martha's Vineyard, sitting by the Rock playing his ukulele. A gathering place for family and friends, it's where we have our cocktails every night at 6 p.m.

alumnus of Exeter and Harvard who later moved to Los Angeles, where he earned undergraduate and graduate degrees from USC and began his business career. He was the polar opposite of Ray, which was fine, of course—just different. The main thing we seemed to have in common at that point was how politely we could handle an engineered friendship. That tide of indifference would take another turn just before I left, when John and I went for an afternoon of golf. I caught him eyeing me, and I confess I did the same; he is a handsome guy. Regardless, we established a nice comfort level, so I was pleased when he asked if he could call me after the trip. As the only two people on the course, away from the studying eyes of our friends, we found ourselves for the first time relaxing and enjoying each other's company for what it was, not what anyone hoped it might be. I began to realize we shared the same values in life—a respect for hard work, family (he's the father of three and grandfather of 14) and healthy living.

Emy Lou and Jerry's instincts were right—John and I did enjoy each other's company. We agreed to meet again at a New Year's Eve party the Baldridges were throwing in New York City. But as John and I kept in touch, talking for long stretches by telephone, the idea of a date in several months seemed like a date in several years. Something would need to be done about that.

John took a gamble and invited me to join him and a couple of friends at a USC/Cal-Berkeley game in San Francisco. I accepted, though I knew I'd need to turn around and within 24 hours fly to India on a trip with Josh. Undeterred, I fed off the adrenaline rush of a secret liaison. One of the trip's best moments happened after taking a cable car to Fisherman's Wharf. During a stroll there, we came upon a guy raising money for charity. "For a $10 donation you may kiss that lady," the man said, catching us by surprise. John took him up on his offer, but did one better. He gave the man $20 and said, "I'll take two kisses." I was charmed.

Another of John's favorite memories is not one of mine, but I'm happy it's one of his. At the next day's football game, neither of us had prepared for rain, which came, of course, and we got soaked. I bravely hung in there, though. John is a certified USC fanatic, so I had no intention of letting a downpour dampen one of the biggest sporting events of the year.

"The gentlemanly thing to do was to escort her to cover, but when I offered, she wouldn't budge," John said. "That's when I realized Mary Ella is a gamer. Every day, she approaches life ready to play, and to win. That's evident by how she's weathered all of her life's storms. She has tremendous spirit."

While John and I acted at first like infatuated teenagers, we matured as a couple during my visit to his home on the Turks and Caicos' Pine Cay. That would be a real turning point in our relationship. Because of the destination's remoteness, John convinced me I'd need to be gone at least six days—in early December, a very busy time for Peacock Alley. I wouldn't be able to sneak off and not be missed. I'd need to fully disclose our romance to Jason and Josh, whom I'd kept mostly in the dark about John. Naturally, they were suspicious. To quell their concerns, I emphasized how trustworthy John was. Emy Lou and Jerry could attest to that. And with a full slate of scheduled activities, our time together would be very proper. Jason and Josh still objected, but I held my ground, or rather, took off to meet John. My sons' worst fears were realized when, upon our arrival, a tropical storm packing 60-mile-per-hour winds and sideways rain forced us to be housebound. I can't say I was too disappointed, though. The period of long days and nights we spent together was bonding, and the stormy weather memorably cozy. Our friendship was steadily deepening, and felt very right.

John and I would reunite at the Baldridges' long-awaited New Year's Eve party in Manhattan. That night, Jerry read "A Friend or Two" out loud:

A FRIEND OR TWO

There's all of pleasure and all of peace
In a friend or two;
And all your troubles may find release
With a friend or two;
It's in the grip of a clasping hand
On native soil or in alien land,
But the world is made—do you understand?
Of a friend or two.

A song to sing, and a crust to share
With a friend or two;
A smile to give and a grief to bear
With a friend or two;
An inglenook to find comfort in,
The gladdest hours that we know begin
With a friend or two.

A little laughter; perhaps some tears
With a friend or two;
The days, the weeks, and the months and years
With a friend or two;
A vale to cross and a hill to climb,
A mock at age and a jeer at time—
The prose of life takes the lilt of rhyme
With a friend or two.

The brother-soul and the brother-heart
Of a friend or two
Make us drift on from the crowd apart,
With a friend or two;

For come days happy or come days sad
We count no hours but the ones made glad
By the hale good times we have ever had
With a friend or two.
Then brim the goblet and quaff the toast
To a friend or two,
For glad the man who can always boast
Of a friend or two;
But fairest sight is a friendly face,
The blithest tread is a friendly pace,
And heaven will be a better place
For a friend or two.

I returned to Dallas radiant with happiness, which put Jason and Josh on red alert. Just who was this Mr. Bitzer? A flight to Pittsburgh would immediately be in order. But John beat them to the punch, making a trip to Dallas. Over a two-hour lunch at The Capital Grille, John got a pretty good grilling himself. It soon became apparent to my sons that John is a man of the highest integrity, and his love for me sincere. John and I became engaged on Valentine's Day 2008. We married seven months later in New York City surrounded by our five children and their spouses, plus a few close friends. After long and happy previous marriages, neither of us could believe we would ever feel such love again. We toasted to each other, and also to matchmakers Emy Lou and Jerry, who somehow saw in us the deep love we had to give and receive.

Little did John know we'd once again be talking strategic planning. This time, he'd have a real stake in it. The year we married, financial turmoil returned to Peacock Alley at the apex of the Great Recession, leaving us with record sales losses. Very simply put, we had another major corporate mess on our hands. On divine cue, John became the consultant we could never have dreamed of hiring. His acclaimed family-business expertise helped us stem the tide of losses with awe-inspiring clarity, and prompted a fine-tuning of our responsibilities and a strengthening of our resolve. Impressed by John's abilities, and realizing our need for strategic leadership, Jason weighed a return to Peacock Alley in 2009.

I was elated, of course; I knew we could make a powerful team. I just didn't want Jason to feel pressured into the move, especially after the immensely trying time he'd had helping us six years earlier. Realizing what a pivotal moment it was, John helped us understand our great fortune to own a revered, 36-year-old brand. He helped us focus on the challenges

we faced, assess our strengths and the potential Peacock Alley really had. Watching John at his leadership best was riveting, but brutal honesty can have its consequences. I wasn't sure if we would walk away as a unified team or decide the family pressure was too great, and that our brand should ultimately be someone else's. But at a critical juncture, Jason and Josh rose to the occasion, announcing they wanted to lead Peacock Alley into the future. I was deeply grateful.

For a mother to see her sons want to carry on the legacy of a business she's devoted her life to is the realization of a dream. In the new role of chairman, I can focus more on our brand's creative refinement and growth rather than the day-to-day details. John leads our advisory board while Jason serves as CEO and Josh as vice president of business development. All are adding vision and vigor. Jason is a true Renaissance man. His flair for perceiving opportunities is unparalleled, as are his analytical skills, which help us see things as they are, not just how we wish them to be.

Peacock Alley, he wisely said, is "the Lexus of luxury linens—not the Ferrari or Bentley. We're smart, achievable, modern elegance." Jason's stellar grasp of technology has led to the revamping of our website for stronger brand marketing and e-commerce, so consumers can more easily stay connected to us there and through social media. Thanks to his modern marketing savvy, our retail stores have seen their clunky sales binders replaced with downloadable PDFs, and our consumer catalogs designed with a fresher, more beautiful look than ever before.

With a sincere style and confident charm, Josh directs key accounts while acting as leader of global product sourcing. He's a true people person, dedicated to the many businesses and personal relationships he has built and sustained through the years. Josh is also an innovator with a playful spirit best exemplified by the "Steel Magnolia," a 1977 Airstream he found in a Texas field and restored to modern-cool splendor. Sleekly American, just like Peacock Alley, the retro RV has transformed the landscape of linen trunk shows, making them fun, flirty and a little cool at the same time. I see Jason and Josh juggling the same pressures I faced, but they'll do fine. Both are great leaders who know that the people around them will be their greatest assets. With interpersonal communication becoming more difficult in this tech-savvy age, they are building superior customer service by hiring people with strong people skills in addition to strong work ethics. They're asking consumers how they really use their linens in these frenetic times—what works and what doesn't—and seeking to provide them with improved products. And, they are both dedicated to strengthening our many business relationships.

Speaking of relationships, though, there's something about Jason and Josh that means more to me than anything: They're great sons, husbands and fathers. I'm proud to have played a role in that, but I give credit to

ABOVE) Josh renovated this vintage 34-foot Airstream and outfitted it with Peacock Alley linens. He has taken it on several cross-country sales trips.

MAKING THE BED

I'm always delighted to hear, "Will you teach me how to make a bed?" It means I've done something right. Here's how I set the perfect stage for sleep.

- You don't need to own the world's most expensive mattress to get a good night's sleep, but I do think you need a good mattress pad. Plush, all-wool lambskin-style ones are my favorite. And I do think you need to change your mattress every 10 to 12 years.

- Keep your sheets freshly laundered and ironed. Always.

- My sheet of choice is a high-thread-count percale, which has a crisp finish. Our 500-thread-count sheets are some of the best on the market.

- I love having a blanket on the bed. I generally use a summer-weight knit cotton, one with wonderful texture for visual interest. If a blanket's rather plain, I'll use a blanket cover. For the ultimate luxury, I'll enlist a heavenly cashmere blanket.

- I adore down duvets, preferring summer-weight ones most of the year. They're so cool and soothing to the touch, and much softer and cozier than standard bedspreads. Personally I love sleeping under a duvet and duvet cover, without a top sheet; it's a much less fussy way to sleep.

- All-down comforters and pillows are my ideal, but as an alternative, I like Ogallala products filled with hypoallergenic milkweed clusters.

- For a more decorative look, especially in guest rooms, I like a lightweight matelassé coverlet. A folded blanket or quilt adds comfort and style.

- I like throw pillows for adding textured layering or seasonal colors, but I do think people can go overboard with the number of pillows they use. Getting into a bed shouldn't be complicated.

Michael, Ray and John for showing them the meaning of true happiness: family.

Three years into our marriage John and I made our home in the heart of Fort Worth, halfway between the Acton farm and Peacock Alley offices in Dallas. "Cowtown"—as some call Fort Worth because of its stockyards—is actually a sophisticated city with impressive downtown living options, walkable shopping, fine dining and world-class arts and cultural activities. John identifies with Fort Worth's no-nonsense style, which reminds him a bit of Pittsburgh. I love that our condo is in the Neil P. Anderson Building, which once housed the old cotton exchange. The exquisitely restored 1922 high-rise attracted us not only because of its architecture, reminiscent of work by Chicago's famed Louis Sullivan, but also because we could customize what was essentially an empty shell within it.

Moving into a condo would mean downsizing, which in turn would mean big adjustments. To compensate, John and I reconfigured the interior to allow for a more open living plan, with a larger kitchen, master bedroom suite, and office space with sleeper sofa. That was easy enough. Defining the décor proved much more challenging, especially since we'd be combining two lifetimes of accumulation into one. To solve that, we agreed to part with many of the belongings we'd sat on for much too long (to the delight of our families, who reaped the benefits of our editing process). Starting with a blank canvas definitely offered our relationship a fresh, healthy start.

We outfitted our home with new, modern-classic pieces that best suit my style as well as John's more traditional tastes. Older collections I haven't been ready to part with, include my grandfather's books as well as

PAGE 223) Our loft in Fort Worth is inside the original Cotton Exchange, built in 1921. (Neil P. Anderson was the president of the cotton exchange.) The wonderful windows with their original glass and the architectural features sold me on the building. The loft was just a shell when we bought it in 2011, and we completely restored it. **LEFT)** From left, Cole, Elise and Grant Needleman.

LEFT) Elise Needleman reading one of my grandfather's books. OPPOSITE AND BELOW) I always bake chocolate chip with brown sugar cookies and lemon squares for my Christmas Tea. PAGE 228) Christmas trifle and cucumber tea sandwiches.

heirloom linens and countless serving pieces, such as Ollie's tea set, a beautiful remembrance of childhood. I keep most of it tucked away during the year, but do bring out some of it each December for a holiday tea I love to host. I continue the decades-old custom despite everyone's increasingly hectic schedules. I think such traditions should never fall by the wayside, especially during the holidays, when stress abounds and we need each other more than ever. During this time of year I favor the quiet simplicity of greenery and candles, and my granddaughters help me set the scene. I'm encouraged to see they have a good eye for design. The boys are equally creative, but way more into basketball than décor at this point.

Two thousand miles away from our Texas condo and farm is another beacon of togetherness—John's family home in Martha's Vineyard. It not only reminds me of my first (well, second) meeting with John, but perfectly reflects the essence of Peacock Alley. It's a place of natural, classic beauty lacking in pretension and unnecessary distractions. The home itself is outfitted in period furniture befitting its 18th century heritage, and complemented, of course, by Peacock Alley bedding.

The home's finely crafted architecture affords water views on three sides, giving the place splendid natural light, and a snug feeling that's comforting even during storms. We feel safe knowing how many generations that house has protected (and thanks to John reinforcing it to the hilt, it should stand for many more generations).

We spend our days there gardening, gathering friends for an afternoon of golf, cooking whatever's fresh, convening for cocktails at 6 at "the rock" (a large formation near the water's edge) and dining indoors at a table for 16. Having so many new friends there has opened a new chapter in my life, one I so appreciate.

LEFT) The original 300-year-old house on Martha's Vineyard isn't winterized, so we built a winter cottage on the back and added a kitchen. It's really very pleasant after all the hot summers I've spent. **NEXT PAGE)** John and I are walking along Lessen Way near the house, spectacular for the trees that arc over us as we pass.

As I look back, and ahead, I'd like to emphasize that this book is not about retirement, which is not on my horizon. This book is about refinement—of both a brand and my life. Revisiting the development of each of them has been a fulfilling way of understanding my family's entrepreneurial roots, my creative inspirations, my personal and professional challenges, my most endearing moments, and what I want for my family, and extended family of coworkers and customers, at Peacock Alley.

And to that, I raise a toast.

May we continue to convey what's at the heart of our brand: classic, enduring style of the highest quality and the best value.

May we forever be fashion leaders, keeping our minds open, empathetic, positive and playful. And may we always nurture others' creativity.

May we have the humility to recognize our strengths and weaknesses, build on the former and address the latter, head-on.

May we surround ourselves with people whose talents complement our own.

May we never fear risk-taking, which gets us ahead in life, nor fear mistakes, which teach us life's most valuable lessons.

May we always be mindful of those who count on us—our customers, our staff, our suppliers and our community.

And may good health and loving family and friends be what we cherish the most.

EPILOGUE

We are very fortunate and proud that our mother overcame her long-standing reluctance to talk about herself and share her legacy on paper. She is extremely humble, to a fault, and the complexities of writing this book has compelled her to reveal both the good and bad of the past. This enlightenment has made us acutely aware of our heritage and what that reveals about the strength in our family. We've had a lot of fun hearing her recollection of a story long ago and then reminding her of the more unpleasant parts. Even when she reaches a dramatic part in her life, she tends to downplay the trials and almost exclusively focus on the happier details. Her resilience has given her the strength to overcome adversity and prosper. We've inherited this incredibly admirable personality trait by example, and we are grateful.

We have learned so much watching our mom nurture and grow Peacock Alley over the first 40 years, and it's our turn now (with her continued guidance and legacy) to take us into the next 40. It is our aspiration to build Peacock Alley into a global lifestyle brand in which we weave the fibers of our mom's heritage into our products and into our family's character for the future.

–Jason and Josh Needleman

BACK) Lucy Ray Needleman
(Josh's daughter), Grant
Needleman (Jason's son),
Jason Needleman, Leslie
Needleman (Jason's wife),
John Bitzer. FRONT) Meredith
Needleman (Josh's wife),
Cole Needleman (Jason's son),
Elise Needleman (Jason's
daughter), Lake Needleman
(Josh's son), Mary Ella (Gabler)
Bitzer, Josh Needleman.
Not pictured, Mary Eloise, age 4.

ACKNOWLEDGMENTS

Special thanks are owed to my dear friends Jane Sobel and Arthur Klonsky, for without their encouragement during the years, this book would not have ever happened. When Arthur suggested I write my story about Peacock Alley, I knew that he and Jane would somehow be a big part of it. Not only do many of their beautiful photographs appear in my book, but they helped me every step of the way, with ideas, inspiration and enthusiasm. They never let me give up, and for that I am grateful.

ACKNOWLEDGMENTS

This book would not have come to fruition without my exceptional team. My coauthor, Denise Gee, was responsible for all of my therapy sessions and for always asking the hard questions. My wonderful editor, Rebecca Sherman, kept us all on track and relatively sane. Kristin Atwell, whom I have worked with for many years, created graphics that reflect the brand that we have become. I am particularly grateful for her discipline and creativity over the years. These people have all become dear friends during this process, encouraging me to keep going and believing in my story from the beginning.

Many friends have been supportive, and Emy Lou and Jerry Baldridge deserve special thanks. They helped develop the book, but most important, have always been my cheerleaders during the roller coaster ride these many years.

I owe much gratitude to my late, beloved Ray Gabler. It was his forever-positive attitude and encouragement that helped me to "carry on." He shared with all of us at Peacock Alley his dynamic personality until the very end.

Thanks also go to my wonderful husband, John Bitzer, who has been there for me every step of the way, not only throughout the process of putting together this book, but during some of the hardest—and best—times for Peacock Alley. John's knowledge, wisdom and vision allowed him to see what we, as a family, could accomplish. He has mentored my sons, Jason and Josh, and me in many nourishing ways. He also makes me feel like I am the most important part of his life every day.

My last and deepest thanks go to Jason and Josh, who have been so supportive during the writing of this book. The years of pleasure they have given me, along with their beautiful wives and families, have made life so worthwhile. My grandchildren are blessed with the confidence and strong genes to carry on this great family legacy.

The photograph on our cover was taken in the 1990s during Peacock Alley's national black-and-white campaign, which was shot by Scogin Mayo. We'd used a model for the ad, which ran with the caption, "Bloom Where You Are Planted." After the shoot was over, we all thought it would be fun for me to get into the flower pot, and Scogin snapped this photo. It was forgotten for the next 20 years until it was unearthed from the archives for this book.

INDEX OF SPECIALTY RETAILERS